Clothes of the Commo
in
Elizabethan and Early Stuart England
1558-1660

Volume 35

The User's Guide

General Editor: Stuart Peachey

Stuart Press
117 Farleigh Road, Backwell, Bristol
1st Edition 2014
Copyright: Historical Management Associates Ltd 2014
ISBN 978-1-85804-288-6

Front Cover:	A farmer and his wife leaving Backwell Parish Church, Somerset in February.
Back Cover Upper:	Dairymaids at Grayhill Farm in July.
Back Cover Lower:	The travelling tailor and residents of Grayhill Farm at work making and repairing clothing and equipment in July.

Contents

Acknowledgements

This series of books is the result of work by a large number of people and institutions. A full list of acknowledgements can be found in volume 34. Pictures have been reproduced with the permission of a number of organizations including the British Library, Ghent University Library, The Folger Library, Oxford University's Ashmolean Museum, The Tate Gallery and the Shakespeare Birthplace Trust.

Preface

This book is unlike any previously published costume book. We recognise the need, from those wishing to make and use replica period clothing, for answers to questions that cannot be answered with certainty and this volume will make simplistic unsupported assertions of fact. It is however only the 35th volume in the series and over 2,000 pages of detailed analysis in the other 34 volumes enables those who wish to check on the sources for the statements to view the uncertainties behind bald statements of fact and obtain greater detail if required.

Beware of standing on the shoulders of Giants,
For oft times they have feet of clay.
Turlough McSween: The Exploding Apostle

If anyone tells you they know for certain the nature of common peoples clothing in Elizabethan and Early Stuart England they are either a charlatan or a fool. The evidence is limited, fragmentary, often unreliable, contradictory and obscure.

Between 2000 and 2008 Stuart Press published a series of books on the clothing of the common people of England. Later, doubts emerged, particularly over the reliability of almost every secondary source, over the terminology used by modern costume historians, over what the period words meant to their users, over the dating of illustrations, the provenance of "surviving" garments and the often circular logic used for dating garments by style. The problem is not confined to secondary sources. The majority of primary material is also corrupt and unreliable.

A new start was required to validate the data. Why does that name go with that object? What is the evidence? What pictures are actually valid representations of the common people of England at this period? What does the original evidence indicate the words mean? Which words can be safely tied to which images? What original garments of common English people survive? Many ideas have become embedded by modern convention and once they take root are harder to eradicate than ground ivy. In many cases illustrations cannot be tied with absolute certainty to a particular period name of a garment or style. New names have been invented for these images and these will be found in Italics in the text.

We set out to collect and validate all the period images from printed material, paintings, plasterwork and other sources, to collect and analyze all transcribed wills and inventories and to inspect and validate the claims of all surviving common people's garments. Only a few hundred of the 25,000 images collected were found to be secure. These form the Corpus Pictorum or body of pictures to be found in Volumes 27-32. Over 18,000 wills and inventories were analyzed which, with miscellaneous other alpha numeric data, form the Mortext, so named as a reminder that most of the material relates to the possessions of people just about to die or who have just died. The analysis of surviving artifacts forms Volume 33.

There is very little hard evidence for 4 to 5 million people's clothing in this 102 year period but by starting from the small amount of relatively safe data we can try to build a possible picture of the clothing of the common folk of England. Along the way in this series we have shown that most of what was once thought to be true is as inconstant as the morning mist.

We ask those who think they know about this subject to put aside your preconceptions before you read this book. Please approach with an open mind.

Introduction

This book aims to identify the clothing of the common people of England in the period from 1558 to 1660 and to make it possible to create plausible, working reconstructions of their garments.

Where
The definition of England includes the subordinate principality of Wales but not the separate kingdoms of Scotland and Ireland, even when they were under the same monarch. This enables a crisply defined boundary of sea and the Scottish border without the muddle of England's recently lost county of Monmouthshire and excludes the need for an examination of residual primitive native costume in the Celtic fringe except where, as with Irish stockings or Scotch caps, there is evidence of their import for wear by Englishmen.

When
The period studied commences with the accession of Queen Elizabeth 1st and continues through the reigns of James 1st, Charles 1st and the Commonwealth terminating at the restoration. The termination coincides with a return of long term royalist exiles and, as far as there is more than a gentle transition in the history of common folk, represents an increased rate of exposure to new continental ideas and fashions across the country. The commencement in 1558 likewise marks the end of the Catholic Marian persecution and the return of English Protestant refuges. It also saw a substantial influx of Huguenot and Low Countries Protestant refugees, including artists and cloth workers, fleeing persecution and then war in the Low Countries and France, bringing new fabric making techniques and styles.

The preceding 25 years from the mid 1530's had been a period of turmoil with the largest redistribution in the nature of land holdings since the Norman conquest, a change, over a significant proportion of the land, from large scale agri-business to smaller farm enterprises and a rise in farmers as opposed to employees in the community. Also associated with the dissolution of the monasteries was the disappearance of the monastic garb of monks, nuns, and friars from the streets of England.

Who
The definition of common people is taken to be those who work to some extent with their hands. Excluded are not only the gentry, squirearcy and above but also the clergy, merchants, bureaucrats and lawyers. Form follows function and those who do not work with their hands, whether it be ploughing or crafting or cooking over a fire, can and apparently do wear different clothing to those who toil. The very poor and indigent, where they can be seen, are however included as common even if unable to work.

The common folk are not a homogeneous group and need to be considered under a series of subdivisions. They can be stratified not only by class, and wealth but also by sex, age and whether urban or rural. There may also be regional variations in costume and clothing associated with specific occupations such as mariners and soldiers.

Chapter 1

The Fabrics

There was a vast array of different fabrics created by using differing raw materials processed, spun, woven and finished in a variety of ways. Without the right fabric it is not possible to produce an accurate replica of a period garment.

Wool Fabrics[1]

The first variable was the coarseness of the fleece and whether it was a shade of white or naturally coloured grey or brown. Sorters even separated parts of the same fleece of different qualities.

The fleece was then prepared for spinning by either carding, which when spun produced a fluffy "woollen" yarn, or combing, which produced a tighter smoother "worsted" yarn with the fibres parallel. Different thicknesses of each type of yarn could be spun and the yarn might then be plied.

Next the yarn was woven. Different yarns might be used in the warp and weft, even producing stripes. Weaves could be plain [one over, one under] or various twills where the weft thread passed over more than one thread.

The cloth was then finished which could involve a range of processes such as degreasing, fulling to produce a compact felted surface, raising the nap with teasels, shearing to give a smooth surface, either hot or cold pressing and so forth.

The combination of all these variables gave a wide range of named products. Although many woollen cloths were regulated by statute the names did not indicate a precise product. The purpose of the regulation was to protect the brand image of high quality luxury exported cloth. At the start of Elizabeth's reign English merchants arrived in Persia, via the north of Norway and Moscow, with camels loaded with broadcloth and kersey. They found London cloth already well known. It had been arriving from the west by Venetians selling it to the Turks, and from the Persian Gulf, brought by Portuguese travelling via South Africa. Like the Rolls Royce these high end luxury English products were consumed by the global elite and rich Englishmen, not by the common people. In some cases, such as the woollen cloth known as cotton, the regulations only applied to fabric of that name above a certain price and cheaper versions were widely used in England.

What did the common people of England use? Archaeological excavations indicate around 80-90% woollen fabrics and only 10-20% worsteds. Of these woollens the overwhelming majority are three fabrics made of coarse, often grey or brown, fleeces, known as Russet, Frieze and Cotton.

---

[1] See Volume 3 for details.

The Relative Use of Wool Fabrics by Common Civilians

Fabric	Occurrence as the outer layer of a garment
Russet	195
Frieze	189
Cotton	17
Broadcloth	9
Kersey	8
Flannel	8
Wadmol	2
Worsted	47
Say	6
Stuffs	4
Chamlet	13
Grograin	9
Buffin	1
Durance	1?
Baize	Linings only
Serge	Linings only
Sackcloth	13
Satin	13
Taffeta	8
Rash	3

The frequency of use of a fabric name in the mortext cannot be immediately assumed to relate to its frequency of occurrence at the period. Garments are described in wills with the addition of the names of fabrics or colours to distinguish them from other garments. If all doublets for example were made from the same fabric there would be no point in mentioning it. Rare fabrics are thus more likely to be mentioned than common ones. Russet must also be treated with caution as it can be a colour as well as a fabric, although likely to be both at the same time. Remember also that the middle class farmers and artisans are vastly over represented in the wills and inventories of common people, compared to labourers.

The table shows clearly that russet and frieze are the main fabrics named for common people's woollen garments. Worsteds occur about 25% as often as either russet or friezes. The next most common is cotton which is underrepresented as it is widely used as a lining fabric which is not included in the table. Those with 13 or less entries, typically exotic items such as chamlets and grograins, satins, and taffetas, are as or more commonly mentioned than broadcloths and kersies, flannel and wadmol, say and sackcloth. Some of these exotics are probably made of silk.

Woolen Fabrics

Russet

Russet is an ambiguous term as it can mean both a fabric weight or a naturally coloured fabric, normally grey/brown but occasionally white or "black". It probably normally means both of these, a fabric and a colour. Russet was a summer weight fabric for gowns and coats. It was widely used for women's petticoats and other woollen garments except kirtles and waistcoats and for men's woollen breeches and cloaks. It was probably fulled to produce a waterproof cloth with no nap.

Frieze and Rug

Frieze was a thick heavily fulled winter weight fabric, probably naturally pigmented in most cases, with the nap raised or frizzed on at least one side improving insulation. Rug was a similar fabric but far less common in England and probably had a much longer nap than frieze. Frieze was widely used for coats, cassocks and gowns, especially for men.

Cotton

Cotton was a 100% wool fabric, cottoning was the process of raising the nap after fulling. It was the same weight as russet but more openly woven making it a good insulator and was mainly used for garment linings, children's clothes and waistcoats. Cottons in dyed colours were not uncommon and many may have been made of coarse white fleeces although grey cottons are also common. Weight and dimensions apply only to finer cottons over 15d per yard, most were cheaper.

Broadcloths

Broadcloths were less common than silk fabrics among common English peoples clothing. They use fine textured white fleeces and were often dyed. They are relatively common with elite servants, soldiers and as charity gowns in London. There were a wide variety of different broadcloths but all were fairly similar. Broadcloth had a dense surface weave with the threads not usually visible. It was stiff and moleskin like. The surface hairs were sheared to give a smooth surface.

Kersies and Dozens

In literature kersies are poor man's broadcloth but in common people's inventories and wills they a rarer than broadcloth. Dozens are kersies made in pieces 12 to 13 feet long. Kersies are found used for stockings which require an open flexible weave to pull on and coats which require a dense thick weatherproof fabric. The term Kersey probably covers a multitude of sins and the common factor making them kersies may be a 2/2 twill weave. Kersies were made from white fleeces of a variety of textures and were often dyed but possibly some were made from natural pigment fleece for checks and greys. They are a fine softish cloth, not very fluffy and with the weave relatively visible.

Flannel and Wadmol

Flannel occurs occasionally in women's garments but is a very obscure fabric sometimes grouped with the imported Icelandic fabric Wadmol and may have some similarities. Wadmol was also only rarely used in England.

Worsted Fabrics

Worsted spun yarn could either be knitted or woven into a wide range of fabrics, probably relatively dense thin and smooth. Woven "worsted" fabric was particularly mentioned for women's apron and kirtles and male jackets.

Say
The small proportion of doublets made from wool are mainly described as worsted or say. Say came in a wide variety of grades.

Grograins, Lyell, Buffins, Camlets, Mocadoes, Rash and Durance.
This is a related group of fabrics which were often made of wool although other fibres such as silk and "camel" [goat] hair can be used. Some were scoured and hot pressed. With all these fabrics their use by common people is limited or suspect.

Some fabrics had a woollen worsted warp and a woollen weft.

Bays
Used for linings particularly on cloaks and military coats. The lower grade bays most likely to be used by the common people used worsted yarn from the coarsest parts of good quality fleeces and woollen yarn from the discards from the worsted combing. Some cottoning raised a nap giving a somewhat fluffy surface.

Serge
Serge was used for military coat linings and a minute proportion of women's gowns and petticoats.

Woollen Fabric Characteristics

Fabric	Fleece	Yarn	Weave	Threads per inch		Weight per sq yd	Width	Thickness
				Warp	Weft			
Russet	Hairy medium	Woollen	Plain	24?	24?	14 oz	36" or 40.5"	Moderate
Frieze	Hairy Medium	Woollen	Plain	8-9	8-9	28 oz	25"-27"	2mm
Cotton	Hairy Medium	Woollen	Plain Open	?	?	14 oz	25"-27"	Mod thick
Broadcloth	Shortwool	Woollen	Plain	56	56	22-24oz	58"-63"	.9-1.3mm
Kersies	Various	Woollen	2/2 Twill	32-48	32-48	12-22oz	36"	0.66-0.88mm
Wadmol	Hairy medium	Woollen	2/2 twill	2-6	4	?	41"?	?
Worsted	Medium or Fine	Worsted	2/2 Twill?	?	?	?	22.5" or 18"	Thin
Say	Generalised Medium	Worsted	Plain or 2:2 Twill	23-26	35-60	11-12oz	22.5" or 18"	Thin?
Grograins	Medium [Longwool]?	Worsted	Plain	?	?	9oz	22.5" or 18"	?
Buffins	Medium [Longwool]?	Worsted	Plain	?	?	11.5oz	22.5" or 18"	?
Bay	Reject Medium	Worsted/ Woollen	Plain	20	20	11-12 oz	45" or 36"?	0.88mm
Serge	Hairy Medium?	Worsted/ Woollen	Twill?	?	?	16oz	various	1-1.1mm

Linens[2]

The term Linen at the period was a catchall term which included fabrics made with flax, hemp and even some Indian cottons. In addition to linens produced in England considerable quantities were imported from Northern France, the Low Countries, Germany, Silesia and Danzig. It is estimated up to 2,000 types of linen were available although not all was for clothing some having other uses such as bed sheets, table linen and sailcloth.

Linens could be bleached [white linens] or "brown" [either unbleached or boiled] although some bought unbleached linens and bleached them themselves[3]. Different grades of linen had different functions. A man's shirt would often be courser than the more visible collar and a lower grade servant might be given brown linen for a shirt while the higher grade got white.[4] There could even be legal restrictions on the linens worn by common people. In 1611 it was decreed that an Apprentice in London "shall not wear in his band either lawn or cambric, but Holland or other linen cloth, not exceeding the price or value of" 60d the ell[5]. A female servant could not "wear any lawn, cambric, tiffany, cobweb lawn or white silkcipres at all either about their neck or otherwise: nor any linen cloth exceeding" the same price. Holland, like other names such as Normandy Canvas, is not a specific cloth type. Some Holland was specified as fine, some course and some brown with vast variation in prices.

While most surviving linen pieces that may have belonged to common people are plain weave some are 2:1 twills. The widths of linens were variable although the widest seem to have been produced for table cloths and most linens for clothing use were between 27 and 40.5 inches wide.

Shirt Linens			Raw material	Width	Weight per sq yd	Threads Per inch
Holland		Fine Circa 60d	Flax	36" min	3 oz	60+?
Oxenburgh	Soldiers Shirts	Fine white	Flax	27"	7.5 oz	50-60?
Lockram	Soldiers Shirts		Hemp	33.75"	6 oz	50-60?
Canvas		Coursest	Hemp	-		
Doublet Linens						
Canvas	Outer			-	14.5 oz	27x27
Canvas	Liner			-		14x24
Interliner		Lose woven	Hemp	-	8 oz	18x18
Breeches	Linings			-		36x48

Interliner:
Various materials were used as interliners but "Interliner" as a named substance was a coarse, open weave hemp fabric.

Right: Interliner visible top right in the Reigate doublet surrounded by the outer canvas.

---

[2] See Volume 4 for 39 pages of evidence and analysis of the various types of linen.
[3] See Volume 4 p12-14 for bleaching methods. Sussex Record Society Vol.68 p27.
[4] See Volume 17
[5] Groc

Other Materials

Silks[6]
Silk was used by common people in England although probably most commonly as stitching thread. By a 1638 law all silks or fabrics including silk imported or made in England had to be at least 21.375 inches wide. Silk fabric was imported from a wide geographical area extending from the Crimea to western Europe as well as being made in England. A large number of fabrics such as Grograins, Chamlets and Rashes could be made either of silk or wool and some taffetas, such as Levant taffeta, which might be assumed to be silk are suspiciously cheap and Caffe or Damaske silk was described as being half silk half thread. The main uses in common peoples clothing was a small proportion of women's aprons and men's jackets.

Buckram
Buckram was mainly imported ready painted and used for bed hangings and a very small amount was used for stiffening the bodies of gowns and overbodies. It may have little relation to the modern material.

Sackcloth
Sackcloth is an uncertain and variable fabric. It could be made of silk, contain white thread or be straw coloured stripped with red. It could be used for beds or sacks as well as doublets. Sacks holding shoes from the wreck of the Mary Rose were made wool while a meal sack in Sussex in 1656 was made of calf skin[7].

Linsey Woolsey
Another fabric of scant conflicting evidence and thus uncertain nature.

Fustian[8]
Fustians were widely used by common people especially for doublets. The term covered a wide variety of fabrics, the more expensive Milan and Naples fustians probably being the preserve of the elite. The cheapest fustians, Jean Fustian[9] and Holmes [Ulm] Fustian, could be made from a variety of materials including wool and cotton and some used by common people were dyed, mostly black although one case of yellow is recorded. Precisely what made a fustian a fustian is uncertain.

Knitting[10]
Knitting was widely practiced and schools existed to teach knitting to the poor. In some cases agricultural maidservants were given wool to make stockings, presumably being expected to spin and knit the wool in their own time. Both woolen and worsted yarns could be used. The main garments produced by knitting were stockings and caps although gloves, waistcoats and detachable sleeves were among other items recorded.

---

[6] See Volume 4 p49-59 and Volume 2
[7] Sussex Record Society Vol.68 p95.
[8] See Volume 5
[9] Possibly the progenitor of modern Jeans material.
[10] See Volume 5

Leather[11]

Leather was widely used not just for footwear, gloves and belts but also, particularly in doublets, breeches and jerkins, as the main fabric.

Animal skins can be turned into leather in three main ways. For shoes and belts these are typically tanned often with bark. For a more supple leather the skin is tawed, treated either with alum or with fish oil. Alum tawing is more vulnerable to leaching out in rain or sweat and oiled leather could be used to line breeches and for breeches pockets.

Leather was produced from a wide variety of species, particularly cattle, and sheep of various ages, plus horse, deer, dog, and goat skins. As well as English animals hides were imported from a wide range of countries from North Africa and Spain to Russia and Prussia

Fur and Skins[12]

Common people's clothes, in the rare cases where any fur was used, were trimmed or lined with native species with the exception of a small amount of budge, an imported sheepskin, on cuffs. This native fur was predominantly farmed rabbit and lamb, although there is a lack of evidence so far for any other use than lining with these. Polecat, probably also domestic, and fox, either wild English or imported, were used to line the front opening and collars. Occasionally squirrel, rat and cat skins may also have been used. Pelts were alum tawed.

A Bristol Freemason in 1594 had "A black Jerkin of sealskin..." and "A Jerkin of spotted sealskin..."[13]. Another sealskin jerkin was mentioned in the will of Thomas Flemynge of Bristol in 1602 although his social status is uncertain[14]. They were probably used as the main external fabric of garments rather than as a trim or lining. Seals could have been obtained from the English coasts or, given the Bristol connection, may have come from Canada or Greenland with the annual cod fishing fleets. Some were imported from Russia.

Felt[15]

Felt seems only to be used for hats and might involve imported European sheep's wool often mixed with English wool.

Stiffening and Padding

Collars were stiffened either with multiple layers of fabric or pasteboard made from layers of rag paper glued together. There is no evidence for the use of whalebone by common people and any form of stiffening except canvas or buckram was prohibited in London in 1611 for women servant's bodies. Stuffing garments with bombast was occasionally recorded. This could be unspun cotton or wool.

Belts and Girdles

Girdles could be made of leather, thread, wool, velvet or silk. They were probably worn around the waist, normally hidden in women by the apron but implied by hanging bags and pouches. In men these are probably the belts seen over doublets and jerkins.

---

[11] See Volume 5
[12] See Volume 5
[13] BW12
[14] BW156
[15] See Volumes 5 and 19

Haberdashery

Thread[16]

Thread came in a wide variety of grades, unbleached, bleached or coloured. The coloured threads recorded included red, yellow, blue and black and coloured cloths could have been sewn with thread of at least similar colour. Coventry blue was a more expensive blue thread possibly dyed on bleached thread rather than on unbleached linen thread.

Silk thread was widely available from rural mercers shops, even in villages and small towns, and was considered appropriate for London apprentices in 1611 for "silk buttons and silk in the buttonholes to his coat, jerkin or doublet"[17] and for soldiers cassocks in 1627 when it was expected to be able to sew 15 silk button holes for 1d. Silk thread was around 20 times the price per pound of normal thread but may have been lighter giving more yards per pound.

Linen thread evidence from Surviving Garments

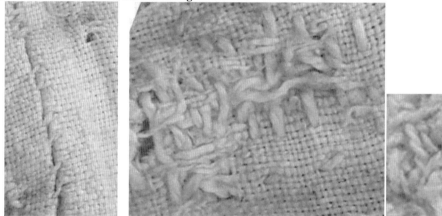

Sittingbourne coif. Left: Original stitching in fine thread about $1/80^{th}$ of an inch diameter.
Centre: Darning stitches in coarser linen thread at least double the thickness.
Right: Enlargement of a darning thread showing that it is plied.

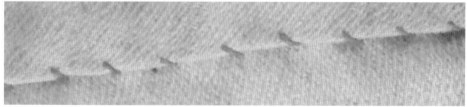

Sittingbourne breeches liner: The thread is coarser than the patches of fabric.

---

[16] See Volume 2
[17] groc

Tape and Ribbons[18]

Inkle

Woven tapes of various materials were available to bind the edges of garments or apply decorative stripes. Inkle was probably linen tape, could be white or coloured red, yellow, blue or black. It came in various widths and finenesses, could have a patterned weave or a fringe and was used probably as strings on some aprons and coifs, as bindings or as gartering.

Cruel and Caddis

Caddas and cruel were probably wool versions of inkle and at least one of them may have been made with worsted yarn.

Ribbon

Silk ribbon was widely available in a variety of colours priced at 2d to 10d per yard probably depending on width and quality. Cotton ribbon cost around 1d per yard while wool, probably worsted type ribbons and ribbons woven from thread were also available. Ribbons were used for points, caps and decoration.

Tape

Tape was made on a frame and its main recorded use is for New Model Army and Elizabethan soldier's coats. Tape was at least sometimes made of cotton and could be coloured.

"Tape" Lace

Lace is a word with two very different meanings in haberdashery, either a tape like a shoe lace or a frilly edging. The tape variety can have two uses either applied flat to a surface as a decoration or as a means of attaching two object or two sides of an object as in a shoe lace. Attachment laces are covered later in the section on attachments. Much "tape" lace was silk but statute lace was a cheaper woolen alternative.

Fringe

Fringe was made on a lyncett frame. Woollen cruel fringe cost 4d per yard but this could be have been used for plough harness rather than women's petticoats. The evidence for fringe on common people's clothes is slight, only one middle class servants petticoat is mentioned.

Estimated length per ounce for lace, fringe and tape

Length per ounce	1 ounce
Cruel fringe	0.5 yards
Silk Fringe	2.4 yards
Inkle	3.4 yards
Cruel	4+ yards
Silk lace	5 yards
Galloon	6.25 yards
Tape	8 yards
Gallonie Binding	8.8 yards
Ordinary Binding lace	12 yards

---

[18] See Volume 2, p14-37

"Frilly" Lace

The most commonly mentioned form of "frilly lace" was bone lace. In 1643 during the civil war Charles the first prohibited royalists of all ranks at court or in the army from wearing "Lace, called bone lace, of silk, or any lace called Bone-lace, or other Laces, Purles, Cut-work, or Needle-work made of Linnen-thread"[19] among other extravagant items in order to help the war effort. The pieces of lace below attached to a letter from between around 1620 and 1654 are probably priced by the yard and with this range of prices are probably bone lace. The letter was written by Elizabeth Isham [1608?-1654] who lived at Lamport Hall, Northamptonshire to her father[20].

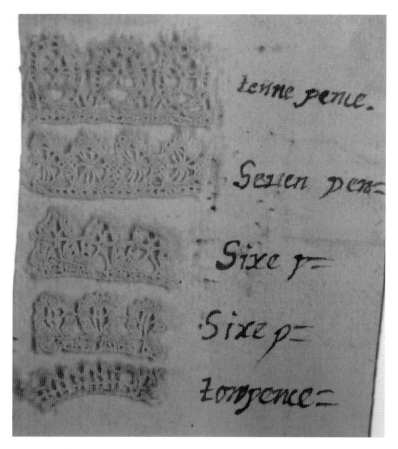

"Lancashire freeholders daughters the finest of them had bone laces or workes about their linens."[21] Freeholders daughter might be Yeoman's daughters but could equally be from the minor gentry and this relatively expensive type of lace was probably restricted to the top strata of common people.

---

[19] 1643 Wing 1629 42
[20] Northamptonshire County Record Office and Lamport Hall Preservation Trust
[21] Life of Adam Martindale Cheetham Soc Vol 4 1845

Attachments

Points and Laces

Points are similar in concept to a new modern shoe lace with its flexible lace with two hard ends or "heads" to aid threading. There seems to have been a choice of material for the lace from leather, silk, thread [probably linen] or caddow [wool[22]], the last three possibly braided threads. The ends were made from a cone or cylinder of latten which might have been either black latten, a brasselike alloy, or white latten which was tin plate. Those found on the Mary Rose [1545] were of a copper alloy sheet indicating black latten. Later latten was specified as metal sheets between $1/64^{th}$ and $1/32^{nd}$ of an inch thick. The term aiglets may normally be reserved for "heads" of bullion.

The metal ends were attached by piercing a hole across the broad end of the metal cone, or an end if a metal cylinder, and the lace material inserted and riveted in. The Mary Rose points had either one or two tiny iron rivets. The ends then were pointed and sharp edges filled off. Workers were expected to produce around 45-50 points in an hour or less than 80 seconds each. A penny bought 5-12 thread points or 1.5-3 silk points. They were widely used by common people particularly to attach breeches to doublets up to the 1620's.

Points appear to come in at least two lengths as with short leather and long leather points. The silk point in the Museum of London was 13 inches long including the metal heads[23]. The lace itself was probably designed to be 12 inches long while the metal ends are just over 1" each. This flat lace is made of 3 strands of cream silk and two of brown, possibly originally black, silk in a chequered pattern. This could be achieved by finger braiding with 5 loops of silk. Such finger braiding, which could have been undertaken by women or child outworkers with no capital equipment, may well have been the system used on many thread and wool points and on laces of similar materials. Other points were probably mono coloured.

Silk Point, Museum of London with detail of the pattern.

Leather points were probably normally made from white tawed sheep's leather although this might be dyed after cutting into strips.

Laces were longer than points but could have "Tagges" set on like the points heads. They may have been used for women's bodies or calf length boots. Leather laces could be used to attach a strip of buttons to a coat.

---

[22] See chapter 2
[23] MoL A12580

Strings

Strings had a range of uses such as band strings, shirts strings and purse strings. Decorative finger braided string making was a pastime among some elite women and a number of manuals survive.[24]

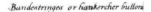

CP1640s[1.19]

Belt Clasps

Reconstruction of Commonwealth Arms Clasp
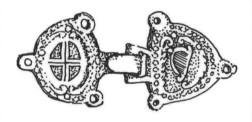
Based on Read No.619-623
Numerous clasps have been discovered, often lost in fields. These are generally undatable but a small number bear the commonwealth arms, designed in 1649 and out of favour after the restoration in 1660. A similar clasp is shown being worn by a jailor on a belt over a coat or doublet.

---

[24] See Volume 2 pages 44-45

Hooks and Eyes

Hooks and eyes were widely used for women's gowns, men's mandillions, cloaks and from the 1620's for attaching breeches to doublets.

Large hooks and eyes have been excavated in Massachusets from the period 1630-1675 about 1.5 inches long made of iron wire 3-4mm thick. These are similar in size to the hooks shown on the lawyers breeches [right] in 1652.

A much smaller hook dated around 1607-1610 made from wire 1mm or less thick was excavated in Virginia, about 20 years before "small hooks and eyes for mandillions" were recorded being sent to colonists in Massachusetts. Captain John Smith was shown in a fight with Indians in Virginia in 1609 wearing a Mandillion. An iron hook about 0.5 inches long and 0.33 inches wide was excavated at Basing House in Hampshire, England[25]. A larger, more complex hook and eye of tinned brass was excavated at Wolstenholmtown, Virginia dated probably circa 1630[26].

Wolstenholmtown hook and eye

Eyes found after the great fire of London 1666

Badges
London Porters wore tin badges to show they were guild members when plying for hire and licenced street traders had cast badges. Painted municipal badges were supplied and worn on straw hats in London for the Midsummer eave procession by paid torch bearers. Servants of elite individuals might wear embroidered badges.

---

[25] Courtesy Alan Turton retired curator of Basing House Museum.
[26] Ivor Noel Hume. 1982. Martins Hundred p85.

Buttons[27]

Buttons are widely illustrated on men's coats, jerkins and doublets and are mentioned on some cloaks. Illustrations of common women wearing garments with buttons are very unusual and may all be of the rare female jerkin. Buttons could be made in a wide variety of ways:

Cloth Buttons Buttons were sometimes made from scraps of cloth. A small piece is rolled into a ball and covered by a second piece. A shank was formed on the rear. This form of button has been found on bog burials from northern Scotland from the late 17th and early 18th century and in Ulster from the first half of the 17th century. Similar buttons from the Mary Rose in 1545 were made from 1" to 1.5" squares of cloth with the ends tucked in to form the "stuffing".	 Replica cloth button
Thread, Hair and Silk Buttons The Reigate doublet buttons are made of linen thread bound round a solid core with a knob on the top. The Abindgon garment buttons[28] and the Maldon coat buttons are needle woven linen thread buttons. Thread and hair seem to be the cheapest buttons held in shops. Cheap silk buttons cost around a third of a penny each and were common in shop stocklists.	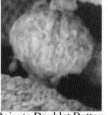 Reigate Doublet Button
Metal Buttons Tin buttons were also provided for poor boys cloth coats and jerkins at Christ's hospital Ipswich in 1597. These buttons were attached with "Lether lacis to sett on the buttones of the boyes cotes"[29] This is probably the normal way of attaching buttons with rigid shanks, such as metal and glass buttons, to cloth or leather garments.	 Some styles of small metal buttons  Metal Buttons secured by leather strip.
Great, Broad or Long Buttons The great majority of buttons on period garments are relatively small but there are a number of indications of buttons of exceptional size or value. The Earl of Essex 30 strong lifeguard during the English Civil War had a gray cassock trimmed with over 180 silver and orange buttons, the neck button alone costing over 12d[30].	 Some examples of large metal buttons

---

[27] See Volume 2 p53-67 for further details.
[28] Abingdon garment details based on Anna Harrisons unpublished thesis.
[29] SufR9/68. See also Vol 1 attaching buttons.
[30] SP28/2b

The Colours of Common Peoples' Clothes.[31]

Only a very limited range of dyes can be shown to have been used by common people. Red was mainly from madder with possibly brazilwood for the stammel reds, woad and indigo, which have the same active dyestuff, for blues and weld or dyers broom, which have the same active dyestuff, for yellows. Black could be achieved by using Green Copperas [ferrous sulphate] with a tannin source such as oak galls or alder bark, while better quality black combined this with dyeing darkly with madder or woad and logwood. Alum mordants were used with the red and yellow dyestuffs. Green was produced by dyeing first blue and then yellow and most of the other shades were achieved by multi-dying cloth with different intensities of the basic dyestuffs.

The colours below were produced on wool with madder, weld and woad in the Green Valley reconstruction of a period dye house and woad house using period techniques.

Country folk were also said to have used buckthorn. These stockings were dyed with fresh buckthorn berries and alum mordant about 25 years earlier. Initially they were a livid curry green verging on fluorescent and have muted with a great deal of wear and washing. The shade depends on the ripeness of the berries and possibly inconsistency of results led to it not being used commercially.

Wool mordanted with alum and dyed with Brazilwood about 25 years ago. Brazil wood is now an endangered species and cannot be legally obtained.

While some stammel reds used cochineal, bastard stammels may have used Brazilwood or a mix of Brazilwood and madder.

---

[31] This section is based on Volume 6

Most common people's clothing was undyed. Woollen fabrics from the wreck of the Mary Rose [which included some elite men as well as the common sailors and soldiers] and from Newcastle indicates about 50% undyed greys and browns, over 25% undyed white and under 25% dyed fabrics. There is also a strong association of "Country Gray" with the 90% of the population who lived in the countryside indicating a concentration of coloured garments among the urban minority.[32]

Examination of over 18,000 wills and inventories revealed 466 garments where the colour of common peoples clothing was mentioned.

Colour	No.		Other additional similar shades					
Black	164	45%						
Red	90	25%	Stammel	9 [2%]	Scarlet	1	Pink	1
Blue	61	17%	Sky	1				
Green	17	5%	French green	1				
Tawney	10	3%						
Violet	9	2%						
Gray	5	1%	Friars Gray	1	Puke	3 [1%]		
Murrey	2	1%						
Purple	2	1%						
Ash	2	1%						
Yellow	1							
Total	364							

[of the missing 102 garments 83 were described as white and others were either brown canvas, which was probably unbleached, or mixed colours such as motley and marble.]

Grey and black garments may or may not be dyed, either can be achieved with natural fleece colours. Black is the colour mention for the largest number of most garments but not for women's petticoats where it forms only 3% of the total or for male legware.

Among the definitely dyed colours two associations stand out. 82% of red and 78% of stammel [a red shade] garments were women's petticoats and 64% of blue garments, excluding aprons, were men's coats. Madder red tends to fade in sunlight while woad blue is relatively unaffected. Women work indoors more than men and this may partially explain the choice of colours. Some men wore blue aprons at work, probably made of easily washable linen. Women's holiday aprons were often in worsted wool fabrics or even occasionally in silk and there seems to be a fashion for green aprons extending from the start of Elizabeth's reign to at least the 1630's[33]. The even more numerous black aprons may be for mourning.

Black may be common among common people not so much because it was fashionable but firstly because black was the default colour that anything could be dyed if it became blotchy when dying a lighter colour and secondly it was the colour of mourning and some black garments went into circulation as bequests for funeral wear.

---

[32] Textiles and Materials of the Common Man and Woman 1580-1660 Stuart Press 2001 p46-7
[33] See Vol 23

The Colours of Common Peoples Garments

Colour:	Black	White	Red	Blue	Green	Tawney	Violet	Stammel	Other
Doublet	36	11					1		1 yellow
	72%	22%					2%		
Male pettycoats		5	1						
		83%	17%						
Male Waistcoats		1	1		1				
		33%	33%		33%				
Jackets	1						2		
	33%						66%		
Jerkins	12	3	1	3	1	1	1		3 gray
	44%	11%		11%	4%	4%	4%		1 French green
Coats	52	8	5	36	5	7	2		1 pink
	41%	7%	4%	29%	4%	6%	2%		1 gray 1 puke
Male Cassocks	2	2							
	50%	50%							
Male Gown	9		1	2	1				2 murrey 1 scarlet 1 gray 1 puke
	44%		6%	13%	6%				
Male Hose	11	15	2	4	2				1 purple
	30%	41%	5%	11%	5%				1 ash
Gallygaskins			1	1			1		1 sky
			25%	25%			25%		
Venetians	1	2		1					1 purple
	17%	33%		17%					1 friars gray
Breeches	4	6		5	1	1	1		
	22%	33%		28%	6%	6%	6%		
Women's Petticoats	3	12	74	2				7	
	3%	12%	75%	2%				7%	
Kirtles	3	3		1	1				
	38%	38%		13%	13%				
Womens Cassocks	5	1							1 puke
	56%	11%							
Womens Gowns	14	4		1	1?		1		
	64%	9%		5%	5%		5%		
Womens Frocks	3								
	75%								
Womens Waistcoats		5	4					2	
		50%	30%					20%	
Aprons	8	5		6	5				1 ash
Totals	**164**	**83**	**90**	**61**	**17**	**10**	**9**	**9**	**23**
	35%	**18%**	**19%**	**13%**	**4%**	**2%**	**2%**	**2%**	**5%**

% are the proportion of that garment in that colour.

The Shades of Blue
The term "blue" is one of the most common words used to describe a garment. 24 samples of period woad dyed fabric survive which show how the intensity of the same dyestuff can produce radically different shades. The term blue applies to the darker shades, azure or sky to sky blues and watchet to pale blues.

British Library: Lansdown Mss. 114

Silk Shades
Silk thread was used by apprentices, and at least proposed to be used for soldiers, for button holes. The same dyes produce different shades on wool than on silk even when dyed together in the same dye bath. Silk was also occasionally used for some common people's garments such as jackets and aprons.

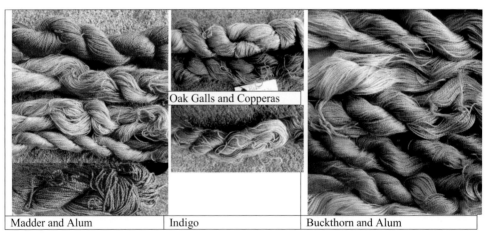

| Madder and Alum | Indigo | Buckthorn and Alum |

Variations with the same dye are mainly caused by differences in the acidity of the dye bath or concentration of dye.

Black: Dyed or Undyed?

 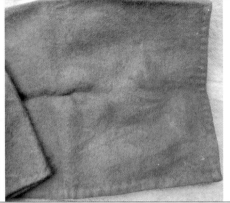

Undyed black russet wool coat with madder dyed lining	A black mourning apron dyed with logwood then oak galls and green copperas in an iron pot

Fading Colours

The Fading of Coloured Garments

It is possible to match the colour of any newly period dyed piece of cloth with modern synthetic dyes. These modern dyes will however have different fading characteristics from the period dyes and the colour patterns will diverge over time and use. A madder dyed coat fades most where the sunlight is most intense, across the shoulders, it fades more across the back than the front as people work bent forward, habitual creases fade less than the neighbouring ridges and under the turned back cuffs and collars fading may be minimal. The coat on the previous page, originally dyed an even orange with madder, has been worn for the equivalent of about 6-12 months use under period conditions.

With green the yellow component fades more than the blue. Many surviving period tapestries have blue grass and leaves where the yellow has faded. In garments there would be differential degrees of blueing in different areas.

Original sources can only take the researcher so far in establishing the colours used at the period. Paintings[34] and surviving samples[35] can change shade over time and changes in the meaning of words make the true original shades uncertain.

The only way to achieve a period colour on a garment that matches its level of wear is to use the original dyestuffs and mordants and then use the garment in a historical manner to allow the period pattern of fading and wear to develop.

In this book almost all the reproductions of period clothing were made either with undyed fabrics, either white or naturally pigmented fleeces, or have been dyed with the period dyestuffs and techniques, mainly madder, woad, weld and buckthorn, mordanted with alum where appropriate. The work was carried out mainly in a specially reconstructed period dyehouse and woadhouse and in the case of buckthorn used berries from trees specially planted for this project. The dyes used will be found listed with each illustration.

---

[34] See pages 30, 46, 95, 106, 126, 134, 135, and 146 for original colour images of common people showing dyed colours achieved. See also volume 6.
[35] See volume 6.

Chapter 2

Who Wore What and When[36]

This chapter examines what constituted a complete set of apparel for common men and women at the period While the basic mix remained the same, clothing styles would have varied over time. Later chapters look at the variations in styles through the period garment by garment. Even for a given profession there would be seasonal variations in clothing and there was no uniformity or mass production so that every individuals clothing would have been moderately different. Many individuals had a number of a specific garment, such as doublets, made from different materials such as leather, canvas and fustian.

Male Clothing

The core of a common man's clothes was a suit comprised of doublet and breeches. Before the 1620's these were laced together with points and after the 1620's they were held together with hooks and eyes. The doublet was composed of at least 3 layers and the outer layer was usually canvas, leather or fustian rather than wool. When they were made of wool it was thin worsted wools not the bulkier woollen spun material. Breeches could be of leather or canvas but were mostly of woollen cloth. In Elizabethan times they were also of three layers of material but later this may reduce to two.

Under this "suit" he wore a shirt of either flax or hemp linen extending below the knees. Once inside a pair of breeches this wrapped around the crutch removing the need for any other underwear. The shirt was the garment in contact with the body and collected the sweat and grime from the flesh. It was washed regularly. Often a detachable collar known as a band was worn unless engaged in heavy manual work.

If the weather was cold the man could wear over his shirt, but under his doublet, a woollen waistcoat tucked into his breeches. These were sometimes issued to soldiers.

Over his doublet he might wear a jerkin. These could have a number of functions, leather jerkins for draymen were for protection while thick woollen frieze jerkins acted like a modern body warmer. Occasionally these might have detachable leather sleeves to protect the arms.

There were a variety of warm woollen garments that could be worn over the top of this ensemble. A simple sleeved coat was the most practical travelling garment. Full length gowns, which did not fasten up down the front, provide all over warmth while stationary, for example in church or while writing, but were impractical in muddy conditions or while working manually. Cassocks and mandillions were variations on coats.

Over all the rest a man might wear a woollen cloak reaching normally down to the bottom of the thigh. Like a gown this was impractical for work and was normally only worn on holidays or if travelling.

Stockings and shoes, or calf length boots for agricultural workers, would be universally worn.

---

[36] This section is based on volumes 8 and 9 which contain over 100 pages of illustrations and inventories organized by occupation.

A Man's Apparel on a Winter Holiday

Dressing for a Holy day such as Sunday a man would first don a clean shirt of good quality linen [top left].

For chilly winter weather he then puts on a waistcoat of warm woolen cotton and thick Irish stockings of frieze. [bottom left].

Next he steps into his canvas doublet and russet breeches, already tied together with points. Over this at the waist is a leather girdle which might also support a purse or pouch. On his feet he wears slip on style vegetable tanned leather shoes. [top right]

Over this he wears a jerkin, in this case a sealskin jerkin-doublet. On his head is a Monmouth cap that has been knitted and then felted. [bottom right]

Around his neck he wears a ruff [opposite page, top left] set with starch and held in shape with many small brass pins.

For total warmth he wears over the whole ensemble a frieze gown lined with baize and furred with fox [opposite page, right]

If the weather was unsettled he would add a russet cloak lined with white baize. [opposite page, bottom left]

Variations in Clothing

The common people were not a homogeneous group, covering everyone from the wealthy yeoman farmer to the crippled urban beggar. They can be subdivided in many ways such as by class, wealth, age, occupation and sex and their clothing would vary accordingly.

Class and Wealth[37]

The separation of middle class and labouring class is defined as between those who are running their own business plus their spouses and children still at home and those who work for a wage. Thus Yeomen and Husbandmen are middle class but agricultural Labourers and artisan Journeymen are labouring class. Within middle class households there would be live in "labouring class" male and female servants working for a wage. Unlike today it would be normal for many to belong to different classes at different stages of their life cycle. Beneath the labouring class lies another major category of the dependant [and criminal] class, composed of the elderly and those disabled, both physically and mentally, alcoholics, petty thieves and the unemployed. Most of these were supported, at least partly, by benefits or charity.

Rank	Number of Families	Number per Family	Number of Persons	Income per Head
Elite or upper class Folk [Non Manual Classes]	6%	Variable	9%	Variable
Common Folk				
Manual Middle Classes				
Yeomen and Husbandmen	310,000	5-7	1,690,000	£8.50-£13
Shopkeepers, Tradesmen, Artizans and Handicrafts	110,000	4-4.5	465,000	£9.50-£10
	31%		40%	
Labouring Class				
Labourers and Outservants	364,000	3.5	1,275,000	£4.50
Common Seamen	50,000	3	150,000	£7
Common Soldiers	3,000	2	7,000	£7
	31%		26%	
Poor/Dependant Class				
Cottagers and Paupers	400,000	3.25	1,300,000	£2
Vagrants, Gypsies, Thieves etc	30,000	1?	30,000?	£2
	32%		25%	

These are crude estimates but indicate that roughly 10% of the population lived in non manual households, 40% in manual middle class and about 25% each in labouring and poor households.

The households in the elite non manual class include live in servants and the majority of occupants of the great houses would have been in service; cooks, gardeners, stable hands, maidservants etc. Many of these, particularly the invisible "hind servants", would probably

---

[37] See Volume 1 for full details and justification.

have dressed as normal common folk although their clothing may have been supplied by employers. Front of house servants might have livery of superior quality. Servants would include not only the sons and daughters of the labouring classes but the children of middle class and even gentry or noble families. The higher the station of the employer the higher the possible status of the servant.

Having a non manual occupation had a number of effects on clothing. Firstly it changed the nature of what was required as the clothes did not have to survive the wear and dirt of manual labour. Secondly the wealth of non manual people allowed them servants to help them dress, wet nurses to avoid the need to be able to breast feed, and the money to purchase expensive fabrics and accessories. A third effect was social pressure where expenditure on clothing was required to maintain status at court or work. Fourthly clothing in winter could need to be more enveloping to keep the wearer warm in a sedentary indoor occupation, for example the gowns worn by lawyers, academics and doctors. Another factor was safety, an upper class woman could wear petticoats made from fabrics that might be a fire risk to a common woman cooking over an open fire. The clothing of the elite, which is better documented and illustrated, does not offer reliable information on what common people wore.

Age
There are differences in clothing for the incontinent babe in arms, the toddler and the child. The other major change in status comes with marriage where there are changes in residence and clothing partly through enhanced status due to becoming the head of a household but also normally through the advent of motherhood for women which required practical changes to their previous dress.

Possible Life Cycle changes in clothing for common people:

The swaddled babe.
The toddler in skirts.
The child [to about age 13].
The servant.
The married householder.
The institutionalised elderly.

Occupational Variations
Certain occupations appear to have specialist clothing. In some cases such as cobblers and barbers this may be a distinctive apron. With sailors it may be a whole form of clothing because of the particular environment they work in and references indicate tarred canvas was a distinguishing item, although the tar may be accidental from contact with tarred cordage. Miners may also have had a variant on normal clothing. Soldiers and servants might in some cases have some distinguishing items of livery or uniform.

The Farmer 1630's

This Northumberland tenant farmer [top and middle left] is described as wearing a grey jerkin and a blue northern bonnet. He has a black box at his waist which may have been a special box for carrying documents given the storey being illustrated but rural workers are commonly shown with bags of various types at their waists. He wears the distinctive calf length boots common on rural workers. The coloured picture of a farmer bottom left shows more clearly a jerkin in a slightly different colour.

CP1633s[1.3a]

CP1633s[1.1a]

CP1610c[1.2b]

The Labourer 1580's

These Late Elizabethan images of labourers show them with full length house and either calf length boots or shoes. The bags may be for carrying food for his midday snack.

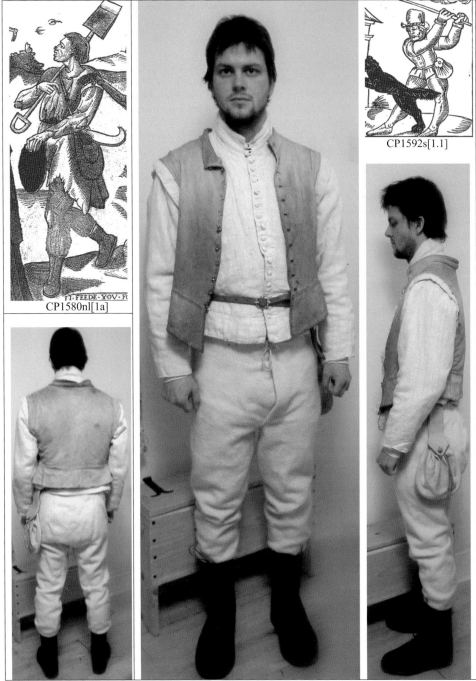

CP1592s[1.1]

CP1580nl[1a]

Ethnic Minorities Clothing

The evidence shows that most ethnic minorities resident in England, from native Americans to African negroes, were dressed in conventional English clothing. Very occasionally pictures show black African pages or Eskimos in their native costume but this is usually as exotics in high class portraits or the first person from a culture being exhibited as a curiosity. European refugees and migrants, mainly protestants from Holland, Belgium and France, arrived in some cities in large numbers and may have retained certain costume traits for up to a generation before assimilating fully into the local clothing culture but the rate of adoption of English clothing was probably not uniform and may have been rapid in a xenophobic culture such as England's where riots against foreigners were not unknown.

The Welsh seem to have dressed in a similar manner to the English and there is no evidence for Scots or Irish in England wearing discernibly different clothing whatever they did at home.

The only ethnic minority in England known to have worn different clothing were Gypsies otherwise called Egyptians. It was recognised in a law passed during the reign of Phillip and Mary that Gypsies wore distinctive clothing and that this was sometimes copied by Englishmen or others: "Egyptian: ...if any person of the age of 14 yeares, or above, shall call himself an Egyptian; or shall bee in the company of such, or shall disguise himself in apparel, speech, or otherwise like such, and shall bee or continue in England one moneth, at one or severall times, it is a felony, without benefit of Clergie."[38]

CP1625nl[2.1]

The gypsy man's clothing appears probably conventional below the waist but he may be wearing some form of headband and has one arm and shoulder bare. The women's clothing includes some conical hats possibly of straw, while others have a small cone or dome with a wide brim and their hair hanging loose below the hat. Others may be bareheaded. Some of the body clothing might be conventional but the right hand woman on the horse appears to be wearing a semi transparent shift and collar.

---

[38] MDCJ280

Regional Variations in England

The population of England was very mobile at the period. Middle and labouring class children left home in their early teens to go into service on farms and in towns but it was recommended not to hire locals as servants "in hyringe of mayde servants yow are ...neaver to hyre such as are too neare theire friends, for occasion is sayd to make a theefe"[39]. The pattern of clothing seems to be almost homogenous with no regional variations, no mention of "West Country breeches" or "Northumberland doublets". There is more mention of foreign designs such as Venetian, Gascoigne and French hose, Irish stockings and Scotch caps.

The one exception appears to be knitted caps and bonnets where a number of regional adjectives appear such as the Monmouth Cap, Northern Blue Bonnet, Wakefield Cap and Richmond Cap. Care however must be exercised as to whether these are worn regionally or merely a product that was originally associated with production in a specific place but is now manufactured and worn across the land. The Monmouth cap is an example of this, being worn not just by people in Monmouthshire, from which even production had moved to Bewdley in Worcestershire by the 1640's, but by sailors, soldiers in Ireland and settlers in America as well as West Country Englishmen.

The Shepherd

Shepherds are commonly illustrated at the period and easy to distinguish by their crooks. Those on the next page represent winter and summer modes The right hand reconstruction wears shirt, canvas doublet and doeskin jerkin topped by a frieze coat lined with warm woolen cotton. His hat is thick knitted and fulled wool and he is ready to withstand wind and cold. The reconstruction bottom left shows a shepherd ready for fine summer weather with a light straw hat and a russet weight white coat. The illustration center right might indicate such a coat or a sleeveless jerkin similar to the farmer on page 30.

Agricultural workers such as shepherds, farmers and agricultural labourers with their households made up the majority of the population. Country clothing was often described as being "country gray" or "russet", that is the colour of undyed naturally gray or brown wool presumably to contrast it with urban dwellers who were more likely to have dyed clothing.

Calf length boots are also seen in most illustrations of male agricultural workers. In woodcuts these along with a long stick and a dog were the cartoon signature for a countryman.

---

[39] HB134

The Shepherd

CP1612s[2.11f]

CP1642s[1c]

Above: Shepherd in winter wear.

Left: Shepherd in summer mode

The Sailor

Sailors travelled in many climates from the Arctic to the tropics and their clothing would have varied. Canvas is commonly mentioned for sailors clothing.

CP1596sr[1]

Right: Sailor in coarse canvas cassock bound with linen tape,

Left: Sailor in woad dyed russet weight woolen cassock lined with weld dyed woolen cotton.

In both cases he has canvas breeches and, knitted woolen stockings, slip on shoes a handkerchief tied as a band around the neck and a knitted madder dyed cap.

The short cassock would allow easy leg movement climbing rigging even if soaked.

CP1611nl[1b]

Cold Weather Wear

Mild Climate Clothing

Where did the Clothes come from[40]?

The women of the household appear to have made most of the linen garments which generally required only straight lines and no complex fitting. Throughout lowland England there was a network of mercer's shops, which could supply linens and haberdashery or even silks, within an hour's walk of the furthest farmhouse. Cloth distribution is less clear, households might have some yards of fabric in store, probably purchased at fairs and markets against future use. Homespun clothing should not be confused with home woven as weaving and finishing required specific skills and large pieces of equipment. Some of the larger households sent out home produced fiber to be spun, woven, dyed and finished or bleached.

For more complex garments, often of wool or leather, the larger farmers at least would be visited by travelling tailors who would make up that year's replacement doublets, breeches, coats and jerkins. Alternatively they could pre order less fitted garments such as cloaks from tailors in town as would the urban dwellers.

There is little evidence of a second hand market for clothes inside England although substantial quantities of second hand clothing, especially shoes, were exported to the continent. With the exception of straw hats the import of clothes from the continent was minimal. Servants occasionally obtained an old or ill fitting garment as part of their wages or more often contracted to be provided with a new garment at the end of a term of service, however it seems that the typical servant, in the normal 10-15 years in service, would receive only one garment in this way out of probably around 150-200 garments worn out in that period. Bequests of items of clothing by dying employers were not uncommon but these were often gifts of fabric to make clothes rather than the owners ex clothes. Where clothes were given they were often specified to be cut up to make different garments, often for children. It should be remembered that employers die only once in a lifetime. It is likely that less than one in a thousand garments worn by servants were discards of the elite and even less for those not in service.

Some London parishes clothed their poor in gowns and shirts and dependant poor in institutions for the elderly or orphans might be clothed by the establishment in uniforms which often reflected the prestige of the givers rather than the status of the recipient. There was also a tradition of giving gowns to a number of poor old men or women to accompany the coffin to burial. As a result some of the poorest in society might have garments, particularly gowns, made with relatively high quality fabrics such as broadcloths although in many cases, particularly away from London, the garments were made of cloth such as frieze and russet appropriate to the poor.

Front of house servants in elite households might also be provided with livery appropriate to their employer's status, often cloaks. Livery coats with badges on the arm were distributed to supporters and employees by the high nobility. These were only a few hundred households nationally and the impact on a population of 4 to 5 million would be minimal.

---

[40] See Volume 7 Chapter 1

Durability and Maintenance[41]

Different garments had different life expectancies:

Male	Duration	
Coat or Cassock	12 Months	
Jerkin	12 months	
Doublet	12 Months	
Breeches	12 Months	
Hat cap	6 months	
Shirt	3 months	2 worn out over 6 months, 1 being worn, 1 in the wash.
Shirt band	3 months	2 worn out over 6 months, 1 being worn, 1 in the wash.
Soldiers Stockings	3 months	
Soldiers shoes	2-3 months	

Female	Duration	
Frieze and Broadcloth Gowns	36 months	Elderly and disabled women and widows, probably winter use only.
Petticoat	12 months	Evidence possibly from an elderly sister
Waistcoat	12 months	Possibly elderly sister
Smock	12 months	Widows
Stockings	12 months	Widows
Shoes	12 months	Widows

The military and the better off typically replace clothing at the end of autumn providing new clothing at its warmest for the winter.

Washing and Repair.

Washing with soap, wringing and hanging of clothes were recognized as an essential part of life and while most washing was probably of linens, woollens were also washed. Starch was required to set ruffs and ruff cuffs and probably used on some bands [detachable linen collars] and coifs.

Clothes were also repaired, often by servants patching their own at night by candlelight in their rooms. Knitted stockings could be re-footed and garments turned, remade inside out to hide the worn and faded outer face.

Shoes were probably mended most, on the larger farms by travelling cobblers. Orphans in Ipswich had their shoes repaired and in some cases almost rebuilt every 6 months.

Some garments were described as turned. The garment was taken apart and reassembled with the concealed inner face of the outer layer now on the outside and the worn and faded outer face now hidden on the inside.

---

[41] See Volume 7

The Butcher

CP1642s[1d] butcher

CP1652s[1.1a] butchers boy

The butcher [right] circa 1640's or 1650's wears a doublet and breeches of oiled leather with pewter buttons, a linen band [collar], a monmouth cap, a canvas apron, freeze stockings and latchet shoes.

The Victuler

The Victuler, a cross between a corner shop and café owner, wears a *mini tab* linen doublet with a small detachable unset ruff and a leather girdle. This is attached with points to Gascon hose over the lower portion of which are worn *trumpet stockings* held up with madder dyed woolen garters tied with a single loop bow. On his feet are *slip on* shoes.

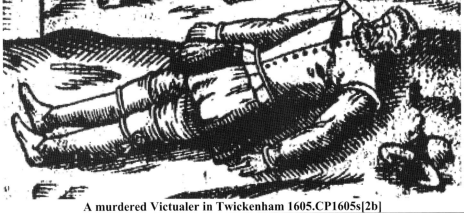

A murdered Victualer in Twickenham 1605.CP1605s[2b]

The Rural Urban Divide

Form follows function. The different requirements of town dwellers and countrymen produces differences in clothing between those who spend time predominately indoors and out and differences in what an individual, be they urban or rural, wears when indoors and out.

Footwear

The calf boot [with a long stick and often a dog] is used in woodcuts as the sign of a farmer while urban workers even porters and other on the streets wear shoes. Farmers may wear shoes for harvesting, an activity only conducted in dry summer conditions and rural women wear shoes as they are normally near buildings if it becomes wet. In one case a shepherdess, who would have been outdoors in all weathers, was provided with startups.[42]

Headwear

Straw hats were made by shepherds and found in farmers inventories[43]. Light and airy yet throwing shade they were useful for harvesting on hot sunny summer days with little wind. Large numbers however were imported into London and some were certainly worn in the capital.

Urban dwellers and country folk are shown wearing fashionable felts or hats. Where brims were inconvenient while working indoors artisans used knitted labourers caps but these are also shown on Northumberland farmers felling trees. In general headwear seems unaffected by the rural urban divide.

Country Gray

There was a clear perception of a difference in appearance between town and country with the emphasis on country gray[44]. This implies a greater proportion of coloured garments in urban areas, which would have generally used fabrics based on white fleeces.

The working environment was different with the countryman often among thorn bushes and briars, which would snag on loose wool, or exposed to the elements or handling wet and muddy animals or equipment. The urban dweller could rapidly shelter from the weather and generally worked indoors out of the sun, wind, rain and mud. His dyed clothes would be less likely to fade rapidly or become muddy. The 3 examples of loose open weave woollen cotton for children's clothes all come from urban environments in the Cities of London, Westminster and Bristol.

The countrywoman's clothing was less subject to environmental determinism. Her roles were primarily around the home, yard and garden. When all hands turned to in the hay and arable harvests the work could only take place on dry days after the dew had evaporated.

---

[42] See Vol. 20 Footwear
[43] See Vol 19 Hats and Caps
[44] See Vol. 3

Women's Clothing

The petticoat with overbody was the woman's equivalent of the man's doublet and breeches. Petticoats for common women were always made of woollen material which posed less of a fire risk than linen. The overbodies might be of similar material or of canvas and laced up the front.

An alternative to a petticoat was a cassock, a full length woollen garment opening down the front to just below the waist. More than one might be worn at a time.

Under these she wore a smock of either flax or hemp linen extending almost to the bottom of the petticoat. There is no evidence that anything was worn beneath the smock. The smock was the garment in contact with the body and collected the sweat and grime from the skin. It would have been washed regularly.

If the weather was cool the woman could wear, either under or over the overbodies a woollen waistcoat. If beneath the overbodies it would have tucked into the petticoat. More than one waistcote might be worn at a time.

Around her waist would be an apron, tied at the front with a single loop bow, hanging nearly to the bottom of the pettycoat. At the waist the petticoat or cassock needed a gap to allow the garment to be donned and the apron preserved the wearer's modesty. These aprons could be plain coarse linens for dirty tasks or finer linens, dyed wools decorated with braid or even silks for holiday use.

In the Elizabethan period she might wear a kercher, a square or triangle of cloth up to a yard square wound in various ways around her head. By the end of the 16th century she might have a cross cloth covering a coif. On top of this a hat could be worn, particularly if travelling.

Over the neck and breast a variety of linen cloths could be worn. A complex neckercher with a ruff, band and body around the neck accompanied by a circular rail around the shoulders or a simple kercher draped casually or carefully folded about neck or shoulders were among the options.

In cold conditions or formal occasions a woollen gown would be worn over the ensemble. This could be closed with hooks and eyes from neck to waist.

On formal occasions some might wear a kirtle under the gown, this came with its own overbody and might be a half kirtle covering only the front of the body. As the kirtle had no front slit an apron was unnecessary.

Over all the rest a woman might wear a short woollen cloak reaching normally down to the bottom of the shoulder blades. Again this was impractical for work and was normally only worn on holidays or if travelling.

Stockings and shoes would be universally worn.

A Farmer's Wife's Clothing for a Mid Winter Holiday.

For a midwinter Sunday a woman would first put on a clean smock of good quality linen [top left]. Her hair is braided and arrainged over the top of her head.

For chilly winter weather she then puts on a waistcoat of warm woolen cotton and warm stockings of cotton [bottom left] in this case both are madder dyed. The waistcoat might optionally open down the front with hooks and eyes. Around her head she winds a yard square kercher of linen.

Next she pulls a russet petticoat with its attached canvas over her head then tightens and ties off the lacing up the front [top right]. On her feet she wears slip on style vegetable tanned leather shoes.

Around her neck and over her chest she now dons a linen neckercher consisting of a small ruff sewn to a neck band and with a body sewn to the bottom of the band. [below right]

Over this she wears a second waistcoat secured down the front with hooks and eyes [top left].

Next she puts on a thick frieze gown fastened from neck to waist with hooks and eyes. The body and sleeves are lined with warm woolen cotton [bottom left].

Over the gown she wears a linen raile over her shoulders and a linen apron which covers the gap in her petticoat [top right] tied off with a single loop bow at the front.

Finally she puts on a hat and if the weather is unsettled a short russet cloak lined with baise [bottom right]. She might also wear gloves or mittens.

Holiday Wear

When people, such as children leaving for apprenticeships, were equipped with clothing they were often described as "double apparelled" which probably meant they were provided with one set of workday clothes and one set of holiday clothes. Richard Garrit of Brightlingsea left "To Richard Padge my tenant 2 ewes and 1 lamb, also if God doth call me, my wife shall see him double arrayed for holyday or workingday"[45]. Similar consideration was given to Women and girls. William Parke, a butterman of Essex in 1576 instructed in his will "To my daughter Anne....my wife to give her double apparel at her going away, meet for such a child"[46].

There are numerous references in wills to clothing used for working days or holidays and in some occurrences to clothing habitually worn to market or at weddings. A pamphlet of 1608 noted that men pawned their holiday breeches to buy lottery tickets[47]. In 1602 Margaret Syon a Bristol widow left "To Anne Sommers her holiday gown"[48] although the exact nature and purpose of such a gown can only be imagined. Holiday garments differ from normal clothing, they were not just the newest set of normal clothing but were made of different materials[49].

The Statute of Caps
In 1571 a parliamentary statute decreed that on all official holidays every male from age 6 and up, excluding gentlemen, were required to wear caps. These caps signified that it was a holiday. The legislation was strengthened in 1573 and only repealed in the 1590's. The type of cap was not specified.

Cloaks

Cloaks are relatively common in inventories but almost no illustrations show common men working in cloaks. Most occupations would find them inconvenient. They were probably holiday wear as Londoners disporting themselves on the Frozen Thames in 1608 include some in cloaks as does the nonconformist meeting in 1641 [right] and lowly London porters going to a lodge meeting.

CP1608s[1]

Gowns
Gowns are moderately common in inventories and wills but almost no illustrations show men working in gowns. The reason may be that these garments were generally reserved for holidays. The cloak and, beneath it in winter, the gown were possibly only donned to proceed on Sundays to church where the cloak, if damp, might be hung in the porch. The wearer wrapped in his dry frieze gown could then endure an interminable sermon in an unheated building in the depths of winter without suffering from hypothermia.

---

[45] EW8/204
[46] EW3/201
[47] STC 2222/19
[48] BW90
[49] See Volume 7 page 40 for detailed evidence for this statement

Nightwear

Some slept naked: "To bed he goes; and Jemy ever used to lye naked, as is the use of a number...stark naked "[50]. A 1641 satirical inventory, of a Welsh "gentleman" lampooning the fact that despite a vast pedigree he is in wealth just a poor farmer, lists "In the bed, two naked bodies, one shirt, one flannel smock at the beds head."[51]

One image may tentatively show night drawers, where a Cornish couple have been apparently roused from bed in a state of semi dress by an unexpected visitor. The man in the centre wears a rather unique garment from waist to above the knee:

CP1618s[1.1]   CP1618s[1.2]

When this couple murder their guest in the night he is shown wearing only a shirt like garment, probably just his daytime shirt.

Rather than the elaborate nightwear of the upper classes, common women appear to wear a smock and a kercher, a simple square of cloth, wrapped round the head:

CP1589s[1b] Witch   CP1605s[2a] Victulers wife

---

[50] Nest of Ninnies [1842 Shakespear Society edition] p 24
[51] 1641 Wing 2574 14

Women at Work

From around 1600 to the 1640's women are often illustrated working in petticoat, laced up overbodies and an apron, sometimes with their sleeves rolled up [See also page 126].

CP1610c[1.2a]

The Farmers Wife

The Dairy Maid

CP1634nl[1]

Right: Madder dyed russet weight petticoat and overbody worn over a smock with an attached frill and linen petticoat with "ears".

Top left: Undyed russet petticoat with canvas overbody, and plain linen smock, coif and apron.

CP1605c[1i]

London street hawker in a white woolen cassock worn over a smock with a frill, a linen apron and a head kercher. The cassock could be done up to the neck with hooks and eyes [bottom left] or not [right and top left]. See also page 139.

The Military-Civilian Divide[52]

While the majority of both military issue and civilian clothing was worn by common people there were significant differences both in the garments worn and particularly the materials used and the colours. Having said that it should be emphasized that this divide affects issued military clothing only, as for many parts of this period, such as the English Civil Wars, and for many formations such as trained bands the majority if not all the soldiers received no issued clothing and would have worn their normal civilian clothes.

Firstly issued military clothing appears to be entirely male. Secondly there is no indication of normal issued clothing, as opposed to armour, being in leather, certainly no references have been found so far to leather breeches or doublets which are common in civilian life.

Many garments do not seem to be worn by the military and there are no issues of jerkins as clothing or any gowns, frocks or cloaks (to infantry) at all. References to military cassocks are common but very rare in civilian life (apart from sailors). The same is true of mandillions, Monmouth caps and monteroes.

Male petticoats have not been found in military accounts to date but waistcoats have.

The fabrics used for military coats include far more of the more expensive coloured broadcloths and kerseys and almost no indication of russet or frieze. The Elizabethan military also used Somerset narrow cloths. Generally military fabrics seem to be mid range on cost, higher than that purchased by common people but lower grade than gentry. In 1627 a quotation for common soldier's cassocks included 120 silk buttons and silk sewn buttonholes.

Soldier's shirts are typically not in the cheapest fabrics such as the canvas most commonly used by common men but in mid range fabrics such a white Osnaburg flax linen and lockram, commonly used for best shirts by the middle classes.

Cotton stockings have been found only in military accounts although both military and civilians used knitted and other fabric stockings.

In general the fabrics mentioned in military accounts are typically those used in the best holiday clothing of the middle classes or even higher. Given the complaints of poor quality clothing made by recipients of the contractors work there may be cause to wonder if the specifications were actually adhered to.

CP1642s[11] looting soldier

---

[52] Military clothing is covered in detail in Vol.25 and 26.

Part 2: Male Garments

Chapter 3

Doublets

Doublets were worn attached to breeches. Prior to the 1620's this was done with about 6 "points" threaded through the waist band of the breeches and through a band about waist level on the inside of the doublet and tied off. This held up the breeches and prevented the two garments from separating which would have allowed a penetrating draft around the kidneys. For a common man dressing without the help of a servant or wife it was virtually impossible to tie the points at the back securely in place while wearing the garment and the evidence from inventories indicates that suits of doublet and breeches could be left secured together and taken on and off like a boiler suit. After the 1620's large hooks on the breeches and eyes, or a leather band, inside the doublet waistband replaced points.

CP1607nl[1a]

CP1652sr[3a]

Where colours are mentioned doublets are overwhelmingly black with around a quarter white and only 4 in any other colour. About half the black doublets were fustian, with a mixture of other fabrics. The white doublets were mainly sackcloth and canvas and may have been bleached. The brown doublets are all canvas and this probably means unbleached. There was no record of coloured leather doublets and these may all be natural coloured. Most doublets did not mention a colour and the vast majority may have been undyed and unbleached:

Colour	Number	% this colour	Fabric colours
Black	37	70%	
White	12	23%	3 Sackcloth, 3 canvas, 1 fustian
Violet	1	2%	1 Cloth
Yellow	1	2%	1 Fustian
Brown	2	4%	All canvas

The one surviving common person's doublet, found concealed in a building in Reigate, is in unbleached canvas and would have been attached to the breeches with points indicating a date no later than the 1620's.

5 main styles of doublet can be identified:

Doublet Style 1: *The Flange* 1560-1620

CP1602c[1k]

A *flange* doublet in white hand woven fustian, interlined with coarse hemp fabric and lined with unbleached linen, worn over a red waistcoat and with natural black venetian breeches.

The collar is stiffened with multiple layers of dense stiff canvas. The cloth buttons are made from scraps of the fustian.

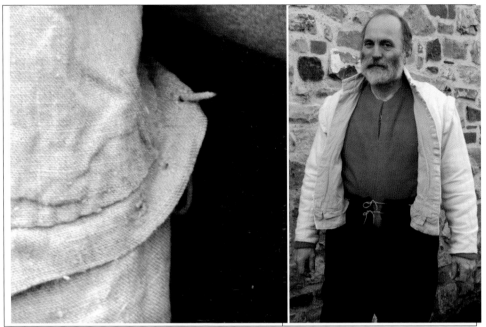

Note the points on the left and right side at the waist coming through the breeches and into the holes in the internal band on the doublet.

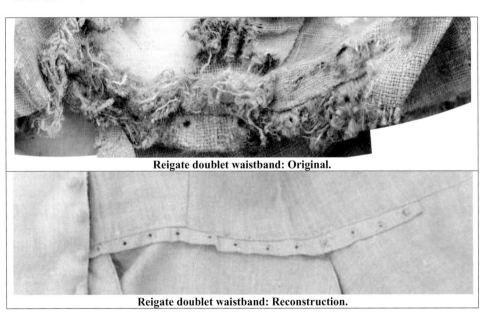

Reigate doublet waistband: Original.

Reigate doublet waistband: Reconstruction.

The internal waist strip has 22 holes about one every inch although only about 12 were required for the points. The excess allowed the matching of any set of breeches to the doublet. Labour accounted for only about 10% of the cost of a garment at the period and the additional labour to make the extra holes was of little consequence even for common people.

Flange Doublet Pattern

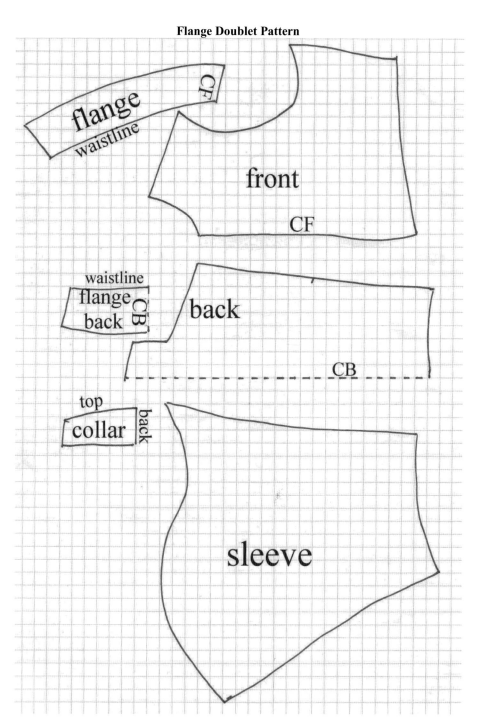

In addition the 2 shoulder wings are made from a rectangle 20" x 3" each of outer fabric and the waistband from a rectangle 39" x 3" of the lining fabric.

Doublet Structure[53]

The bodies of all doublets have at least three layers, the outer material, an inner liner and sandwiched between them an interliner. In the case of the Reigate doublet the interliner was a coarse loosely woven hemp material. If the outer layer was ornamentally slashed then a fourth decorative layer might have been added between the outer and the interliner, possibly dyed silk, but this was probably not present in the vast majority of common people's doublets. Without an interliner the body of a doublet behaves in a very different manner in terms of warmth and the way it hangs.

The sleeves of the Reigate doublet were not interlined and some doublets had sleeves in different materials to the bodies.

Back Construction

Some doublets have a seam down the centre of the back which can be seen in some illustrations [left].

The Reigate doublet in contrast has two fore parts but only a single piece back which reaches up to the top of the collar a style which can be seen in some early illustrations [right]. [This is probably not a picture of a doublet but is a similar collar construction].

CP1637nlo[2.5a]

CP1562s[1]

Some doublets have wings and others do not, some wings are decorated but most are plain.

Stuffing and Stiffening.
Collars were stiffened either with multiple layers of canvas or pasteboard. The V and A doublet has pastboard belly pieces but this may be borderline elite. Some soldier's doublets were stuffed with bombast.

Girdles
Many doublets are shown with a thin belt around the waist. This was probably termed a girdle and for common men could be made of leather, braided fabric or even silk.

Buttons
The London Apprentice in 1611 was prohibited from using silk with the specific exception of "silk buttons and silk in the buttonholes to his coat, jerkin or doublet." Cheaper buttons could be made with thread or hair or be metal or cloth[54].

Binding
Some illustrations show a stripe up the front opening of the doublet. This is probably binding tape or lists cut from the edges of woolen fabric.

---

[53] See Volumes 10 and 11 for full details on doublets
[54] See Page 18 or Volume 2 Haberdashery for fuller details.

The Reigate Doublet [Probably first quarter 17th century]

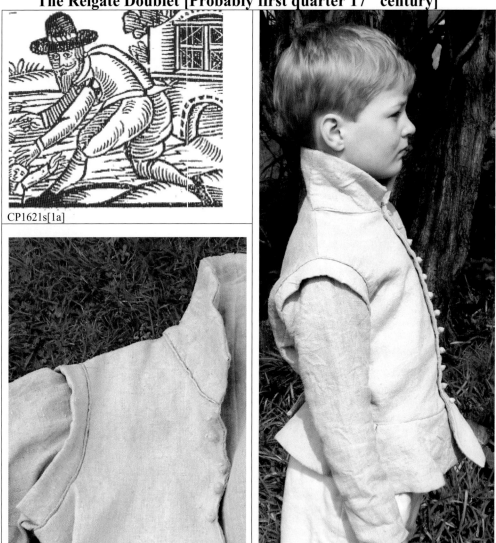

CP1621s[1a]

Note the details of shoulder and neck piping	The original would have fitted a nine year old boy

A reconstruction of the Reigate doublet with the outer face of close, even weave, unbleached canvas, the lining of close, even weave, unbleached canvas, slightly coarse than the outer. The interliner was of coarse, open weave, hemp material. The buttons were of thread bound round a wooden core. The neck was stiffened with multiple layers of canvas.

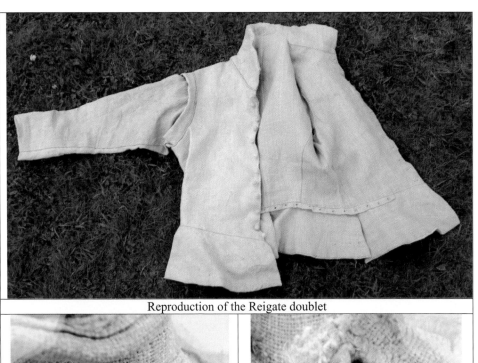

Reproduction of the Reigate doublet

Collar and neck piping on the original | Button hole on original

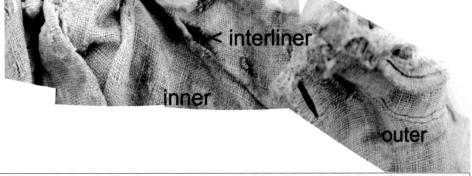

The multiple layers of the remains of the original Reigate Doublet which was found crumpled and hidden next to the chimney of a shop.

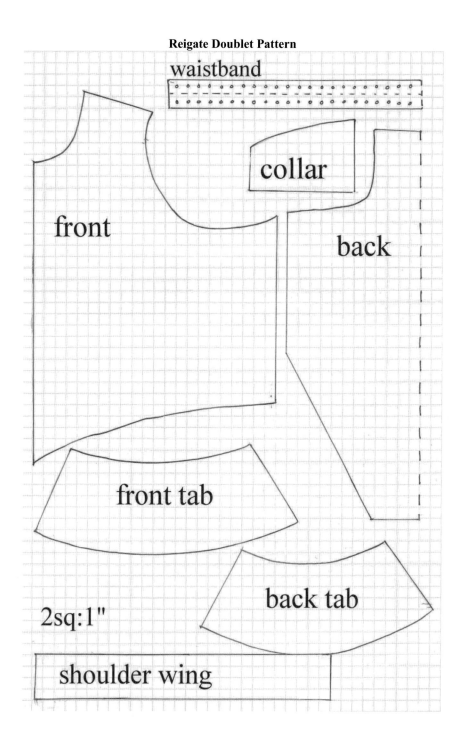

waistband

collar

front

back

front tab

back tab

2sq:1"

shoulder wing

Reigate Doublet Pattern: Sleeves and Piping

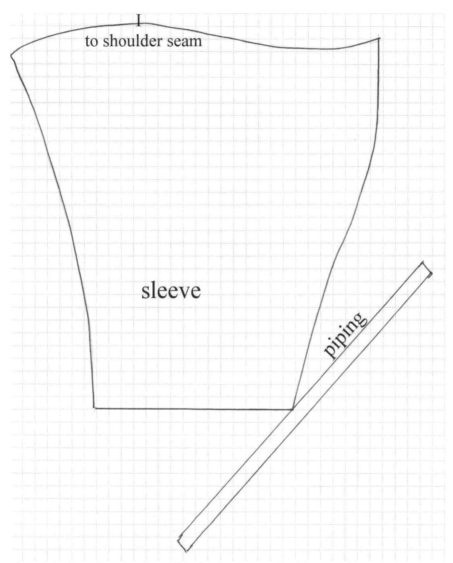

to shoulder seam

sleeve

piping

The original was found to fit a child of 9 about 5'3" tall with a 28" chest.

The reproduction has a 3 panel body with the collar cut in with back panel. It has 12 buttons up the front plus one on the collar, welted neck and arm hole seams and the collar stiffening was 3 layers of interlining. The body is interlined but not the sleeves and there are 22 one inch spaced eyelets for lacing to breeches on the internal waistband.

Doublet Style 3: *Mini Tab* Doublet 1605-1626

Mini Tab doublet in unbleached canvas with points, three panel body and curved sleeves. Piping along the neck and arm hole seams. Lined with unbleached linen and interlined with coarse hemp interliner. The neck is stiffened with multiple layers of interliner. Worn with a leather girdle.

CP1608s[2c]	Note the attachment of the breeches to doublet with points through the internal waist band.

Doublet Materials

Doublets were made from a wide variety of materials, the main being varieties of leather, fustians, and canvas which account for 76% of the total. Various woven woolen fabrics account for only 14% and these are mostly thin, combed, worsted types. Luxury fabrics, adding in the expensive Milan fustians to the satins and silks, account for 11%.

Doublet Materials	No.	%	Notes
Leather	80	**34%**	30% where specified deer
Canvas	54	**23%**	6% specified white, 2% brown, 6% specified cut.
Fustian	45	**19%**	29% specified black.
Woven Wool	33	**14%**	
Worsted type wools	14	6%	Worsted 11, Say 1, Stuff 2
Sackcloth	11	5%	44% specified white.
Cloth	6	3%	33% specified black
Kersey	2	1%	
Knitted	1	**0.5%**	
Satin	13	**6%**	
Silk etc	11	**5%**	Grograin 4, Chamlet 1, Rash 4, Taffetta 1, Damask 1.
Total	**237**		

Woollen doublets are overwhelmingly owned by non agriculturally based men while canvas, leather and fustian doublets are mostly owned by those working in agriculture [Yeomen, Husbandmen and Labourers]. Luxury materials are mostly worn by non agricultural men. In many cases men were recorded with a number of doublets of different materials.

Mini Tab **Doublet Pattern**

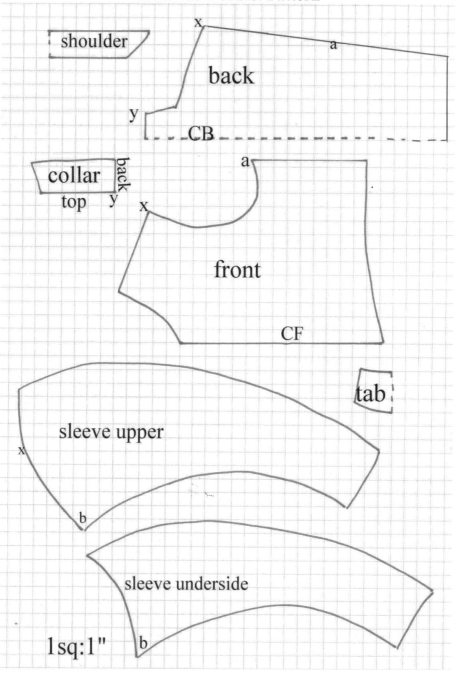

In addition the waistband is made from a rectangle 43" x 3" of strong linen fabric and welting strips were cut on the cross as in the Reigate pattern for the neck and armholes.

By the mid 1620's doublets had appeared with a smaller number of large tabs. Two styles are shown with either 6 or 8 tabs. Type 4 has a front that is horizontal across the waist and the bottom of the tabs, Type 5 is pointed downwards in these areas.

Doublet Type 4: 6 Tab Doublet 1625-1647

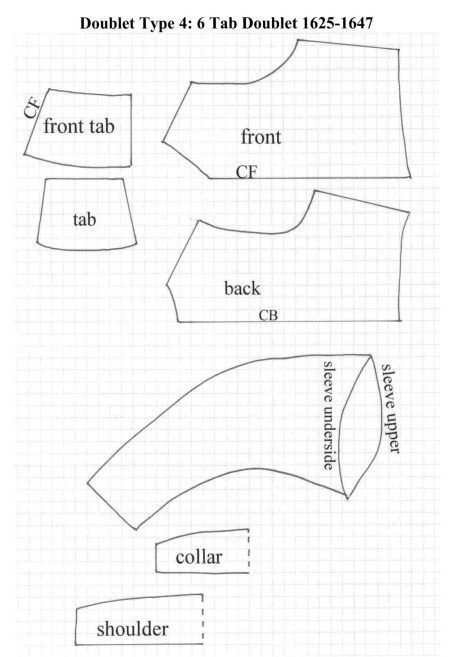

In addition a pieced strip of leather 1" wide and 41" long is required for the waist strip and about a further 150" of 1" strip will be required for welting the shoulder seams and tab edges.

Doublet Type 4: 6 Tab Doublet 1625-1647

6 tab doublet with 4 panel body in oiled deerskin outer and liner with hemp interliner and pewter buttons. The sleeves are lined with canvas. The shoulder seams and the edges of the tabs are piped with leather. The Breeches hook to a leather strip around the inside of the waist.

8 Tab Pointed Doublet 1625-1647

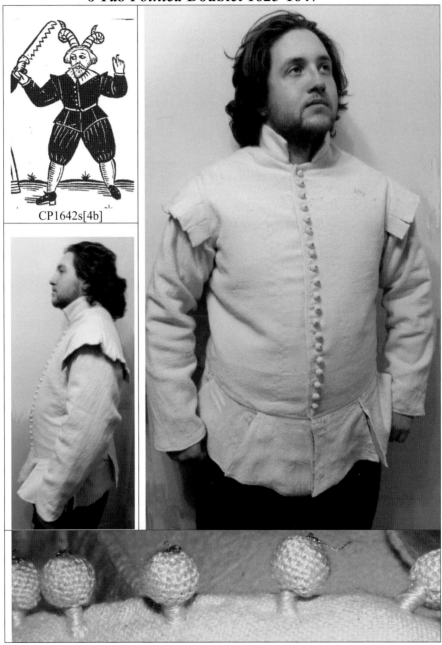

CP1642s[4b]

8 tab jean [linen/cotton] fustian doublet with hooks and eyes on the internal waistband, interlined with coarse hemp. The buttons are of silk worked on a wooden core sewn on with heavy linen bound at the top with copper wire. Note the shoulder pieces are made from strips of fustian about 1.5 inches wide.

Pattern for 8 Tab Doublet

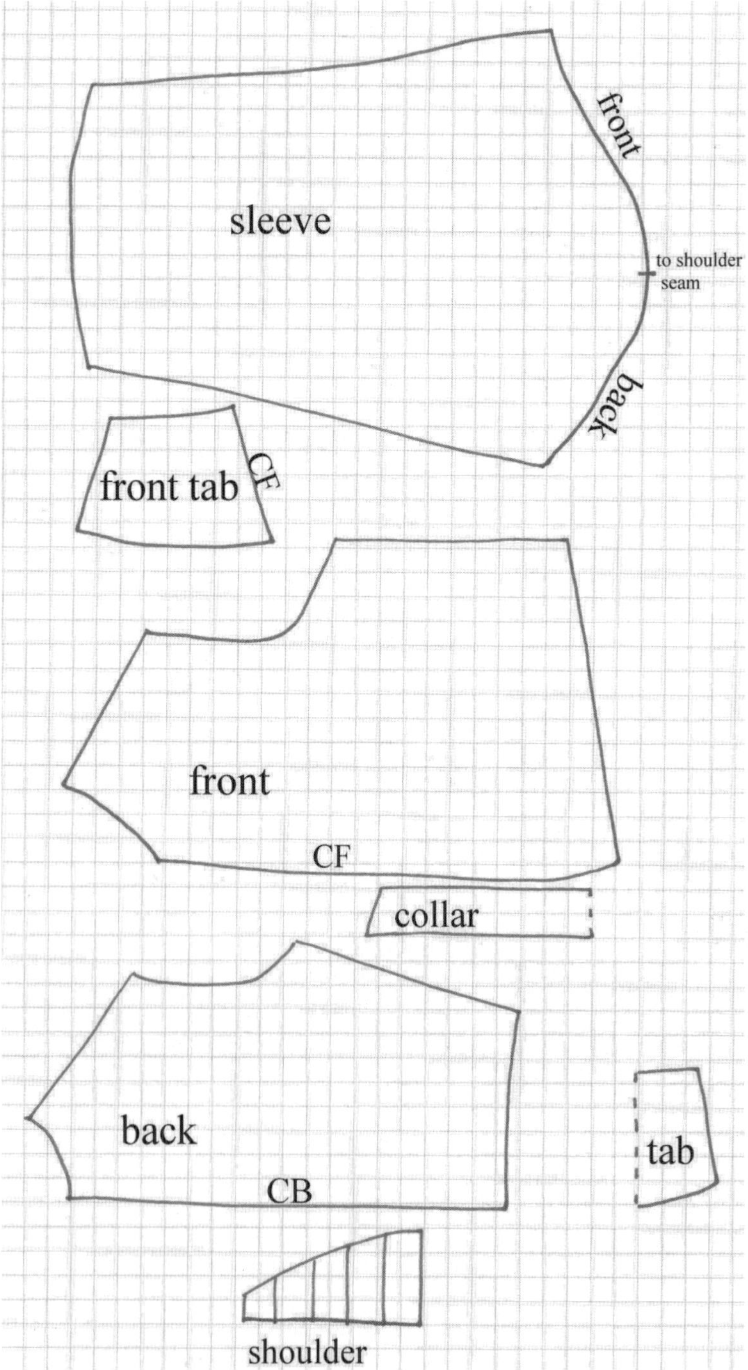

sleeve

front

to shoulder seam

back

front tab

CF

front

CF

collar

back

CB

tab

shoulder

Scale 1 square to 1". An addition 42" by 3" strip of linen is required for the waistband, to which the eyes are sewn.

Chapter 4
Male Legwear

Sometimes known as breeches and sometimes as hose these were the most varied and complex of garments over the Elizabethan and Early Stuart period. Hose may include some garments we would today call stockings as well as what we would now call breeches. The fabrics used for common peoples "hose" and breeches are generally similar, the knit and silk hose may be "stockings" rather than breeches style hose. In broad terms nearly two thirds are of woollen materials, a fifth to a third of leather and just under a tenth of vegetable fibre.

Hose Fabrics			Breeches Fabric			
Woolen Cloth		**63%**	**Woollen**	29	**59%**	
Russet	31	50%	Russet	14	29%	3 white, 1 black, 1blue
Frieze	2	3%	Frieze	8	16%	1 white, 1 black
Kersey	3	5%	Kersey	1	2%	
Worsted	1	2%	Stuff	1	2%	
Buffin	1	2%	Grograin	1	2%	
			Broadcloth	1	2%	Russet
Cloth	3	5%	Unspecified Wool	3	6%	
Knitt	4	**6%**	**Knit**	-		
Leather		**20%**	**Leather**	16	**33%**	
Unspecified leather	4	6%	Unspecified leather	7	14%	
Buff	7	11%	Buff	2	4%	
Doeskin	1	2%	-	-	-	
Bucks leather	1	2%	Bucks leather	7	14%	
Vegetable fibre		**9%**	**Vegetable fibre**		**8%**	
Linen	3	3%	Linen	1	2%	
Canvas	1	2%	Canvas	3	6%	1 white
Fustian	2	3%				
Silk	2	**3%**	**Silk**	-		

Where a colour is mentioned most are russet, white or black which were definitely or could be undyed. Probably only a small proportion of breeches were dyed.

Hose Colours				Breeches colours			
Russet	31			Russet	14	Possibly undyed fabric rather than a colour	
White	16	40%		White	6	32%	Undyed
Black	13	33%		Black	4	21%	Possibly some from black fleece
Blue	4	10%	1 sky	Blue	6	32%	1 russet
Green	2	5%		Green	1	5%	
Red	2	5%					
Purple	1	3%					
Ash	1	3%		Tawney	1	5%	
Motley	1	3%		Violet	1	5%	
There is no indication that any of the leather hose or breeches were dyed and the vast majority were probably undyed.							

Linings

Elizabethan hose are typically made of three layers consisting of an outer material as above, a linen inner liner and sandwiched between an interliner commonly of woollen cotton. By the 17th century mention of interlinings disappears and breeches probably consist of two layers. By this time oiled leather linings for breeches are mentioned as well as linen liners.

The Sittingbourne Breeches Liner The main fabric is a natural colour, plain weave, linen or hemp. The threads in the weft are somewhat variable in thickness.	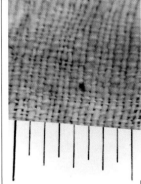	

Breeches Pockets [55]

Pockets were widespread in common peoples breeches in the 17th century although there is no evidence in the 16th century. Pairs of leather pockets were used for thousands of military breeches in the 1640's. A pair of breeches of uncertain social status in the V&A has pockets made of a chamois style leather.
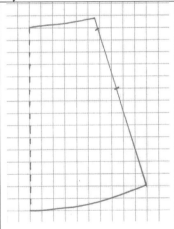 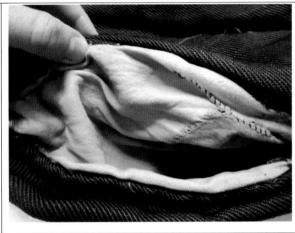
Pattern for a pocket based on the V and A breeches leather pocket.   1 sq = 1 inch
Step 1: Piece together pieces of leather and trim to form the pattern shape above. Size is not precise at around 14 inches top to bottom, 20 inches wide at the bottom and 13 inches wide at the top. The bottom line is slightly curved. Step 2: Sew above and below the pocket opening [marked by dashes on the right hand side of pattern]. Step 3: Fold so that the seam is in the centre. Sew across the bottom edge of the pocket. Step 4: Stitch the pocket into the opening of the breeches. Step 5: Attach top of pocket to waistband seam of breeches, gathering if necessary.

---

[55] See Volume 16

Overbreeches and Night Drawers

One specialist sub group of breeches were known as slivers or drawers. Half of these were made of the woollen materials cotton and russet and were for drawing on over normal breeches when riding, along with a riding coat to keep the mud kicked up by horse's hoofs off one's clothes. The other half were made of linen and there are indications that these are a form of pyjama bottom for wearing in bed.

Male Night Drawers

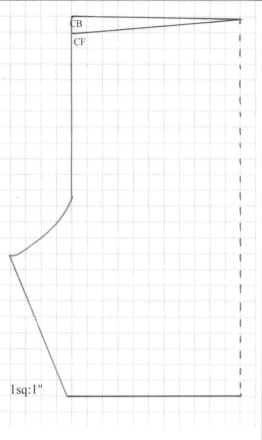

1 sq:1"

CB

CF

English merchant in Indonesia 1624 being waterboarded by the Dutch

Depending on the width of fabric and wearer an additional seam may be necessary. The waist is gathered onto a piece of linen tape leaving an inch before the centre front to allow for a slight overlap at the flies.

In some cases the edge at the bottom of the leg may be gathered onto a band which may be tied.

Holding Up Breeches

	The upper portion of male legware at the period was apparently normally attached to the doublet although this may be less absolute towards the very end of the period under study. The attachment helped suspend the breeches or hose at waist height but was not essential to keep the legware from falling as men involved in hot, strenuous work are sometimes shown without a doublet:	
CP1652sr[3a]		CP1633s[1.1a]

Prior to the 1620's breeches were attached to doublets with points, after the 1620's this was with hooks as above left.

Buttons on Breeches.

Fly buttons are not visible on illustrations of common men's clothing however the Sittingbourne breeches liner shows tufts from 9 buttons. Early Elizabethan slops [see page 74] show the opening at the bottom of the leg closed with two buttons and a looting soldier in Ireland[56] has his breeches decorated with buttons although this picture is unique.

Ornamentation

	Breeches could be decorated with guards or lace. A number of post 1600 illustrations of breeches have a stripe up the side.	
CP1618s[2a]		CP1619sr[2a]

For clarity the following illustrations of reproductions of pairs of breeches have been shown without attached doublets. The breeches illustrated thus have less upward support and may slump slightly compared to their normal position.

---

[56] See page 48

Men in Tights Pattern.

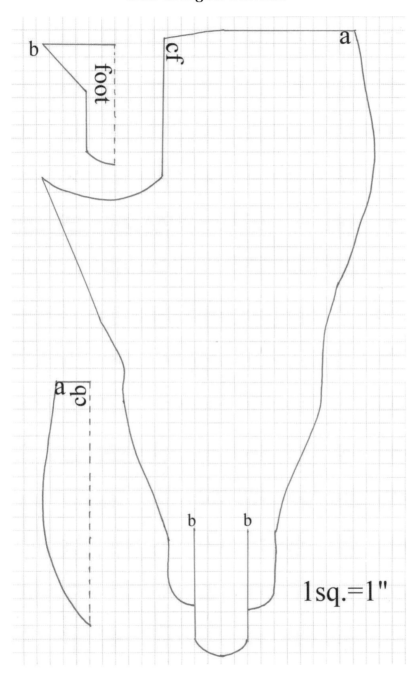

Cut a strip of canvas to interline the top of the hose to strengthen the area where the points are attached.

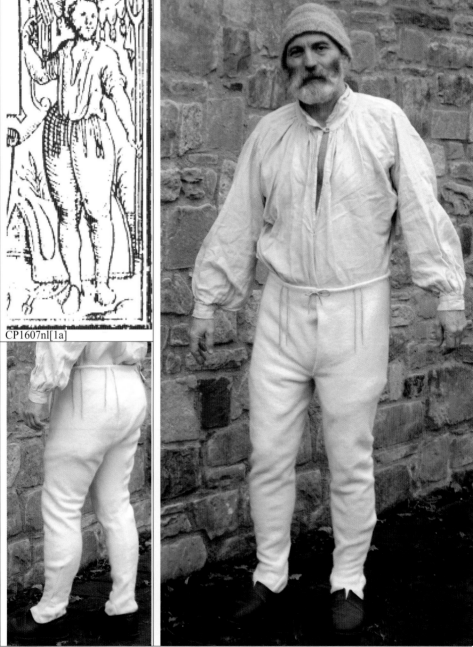

CP1607nl[1a]

Full length hose, including a foot, in white open weave kersey. They are unlined but the waistband is double thickness with a canvas interliner to support the points attaching the hose to the doublet. Closed at the waist with points

Chav Breeches 1550's to early 1560's

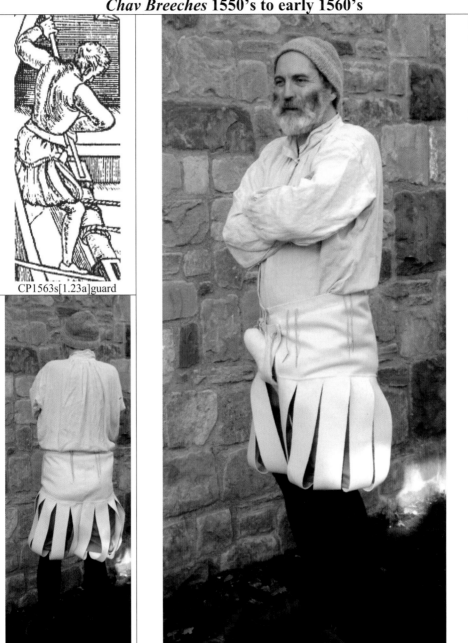

CP1563s[1.23a]guard

In white kersey with an inner liner of linen and interlined with grey cotton. In addition the kersey outer is backed, only in the slit panes, with a visible lining of buckthorn dyed green fustian. Points are used to secure the codpiece flap and to attach the breeches to the doublet.

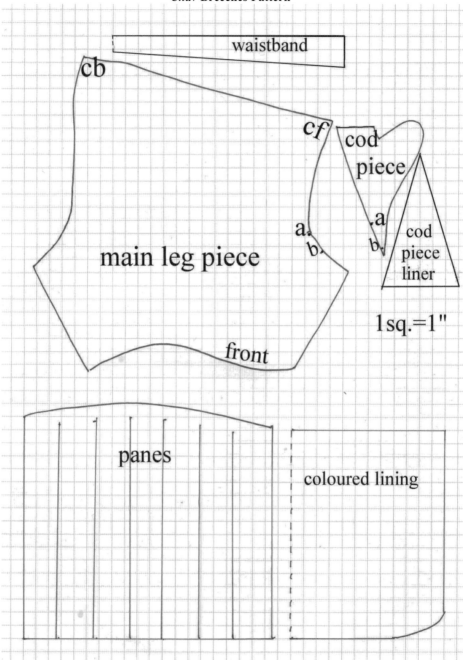

waistband

cb

cf

cod piece

a

b

a

b

cod piece liner

main leg piece

front

1sq.=1"

panes

coloured lining

The triangular piece forms the inside face of the codpiece.

In addition cut a waistband interliner from canvas.

Slops 1558-1560's and 1650's

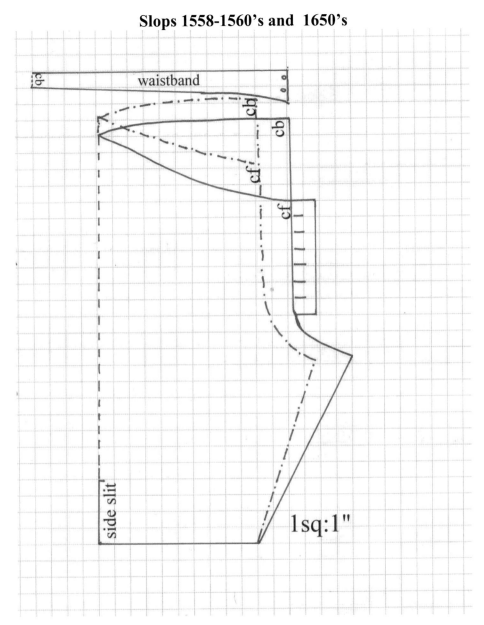

In addition a canvas interliner for the waistband should be cut [without seam allowance but otherwise the same size and shape as the waistband]. The waistband is made of the same woollen material as the outer.

The linen linings go to the top of the waistband and the points are worked through all layers.

The above pattern is based on the 1560's but a very similar garment without the side opening at the bottom of the leg appears in the 1650's

Slops 1558-1560's and 1650's

CP1563s[1.20b]guard

Slops in woad dyed russet weight fabric, lined with linen.

Round Hose 1580's-1590's [possibly also 1570's]

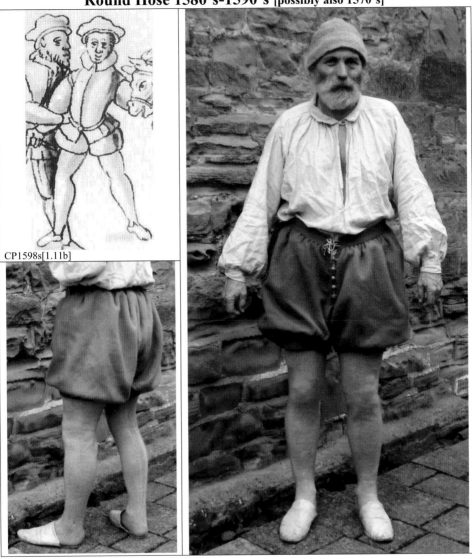

CP1598s[1.11b]

Round hose in russet weight cloth dyed green with weld and woad, interlined in the upper part with russet and lined with linen.

The woad dyed knitted nether hose are from the Gunnister pattern[57]. The method of attachment of the netherstocks is uncertain. Possibilities include that they might be sewn on, attached with points or be the exposed part of full length tights.

---

[57] See Vol. 18

Round Hose Pattern

The outer fabric pattern

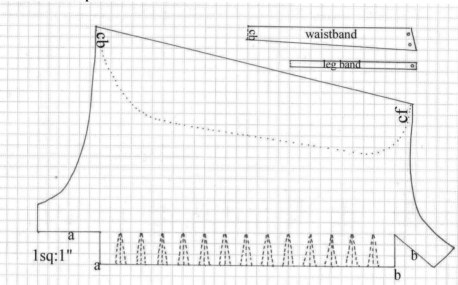

The dotted line represents the edge of the woollen interliner. The waistband is interlined with heavy canvas. The darts at the bottom of the leg are folded and sewn so that the fold is inside the garment.

The lining pattern

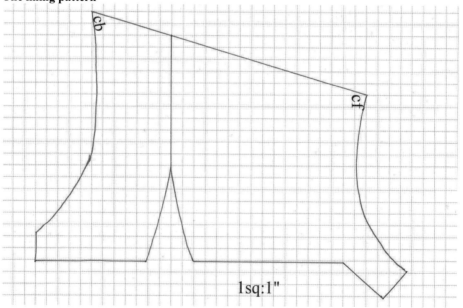

Uncommon French Hose 1580's

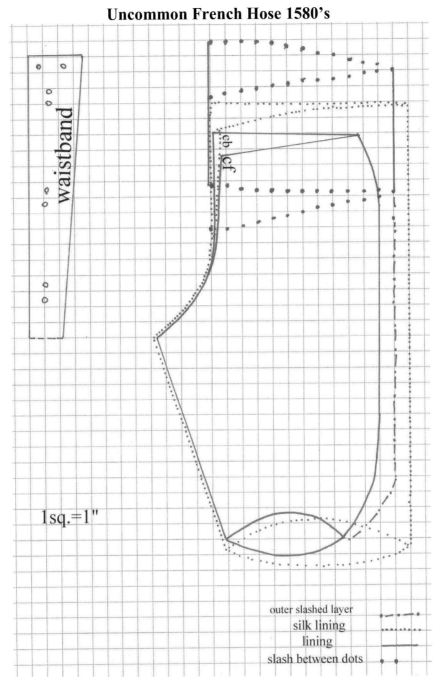

waistband

1 sq.=1"

eb cf

outer slashed layer	– · – · – ·
silk lining	· · · · · · · · ·
lining	——————
slash between dots	· — · — ·

Cut a waistband interliner from canvas.

The Cotton interliner needs to be cut slightly wider than the liner [except at the bottom of the leg where it should be slightly shorter] so that they lie smoothly together.

77

Uncommon French Hose 1580's

London Trained Band Pikemen at a state funeral in 1586. CP1587s[1.2f]

Madder dyed orange say lined with woad dyed watchet silk and the strips backed with buckthorn dyed sage green fustian. The hose are interlined with cotton and lined with linen. The inside of the bottom of the leg is fastened with a hook and eye.

Deflater Hose

Early Deflater Hose or Galligaskins mid 1570's? or 1590's to circa 1605.
Later Deflater Hose Circa 1605 to mid 1610's possibly mid 1620's

CP1608s[1a]

Later deflater hose in gray russet with a linen lining, with points.
In early deflater hose the top of the lower portion of the leg is wider, tapering more.

Later Deflater Hose Pattern

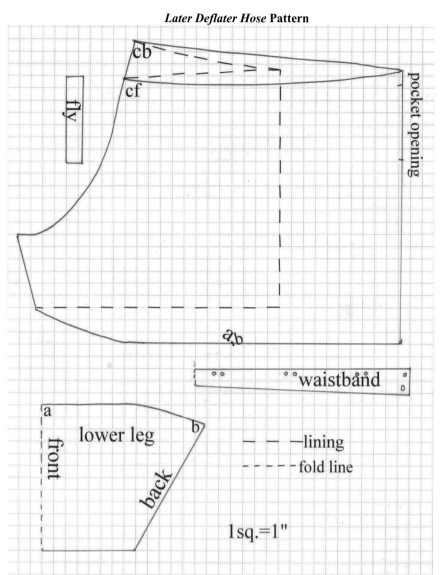

Cut a linen liner for each part. The liner for the upper part does not need to be as wide as the outer cloth.

Cut a canvas interliner for the waistband.

The leg part goes around the lower thigh [bottom left piece]. The seam should align with the centre back of the leg when attaching to the gathered upper part.

Period illustrations indicate variations in proportions between the upper and lower parts and the tightness of the lower part.

Venetians Patterns

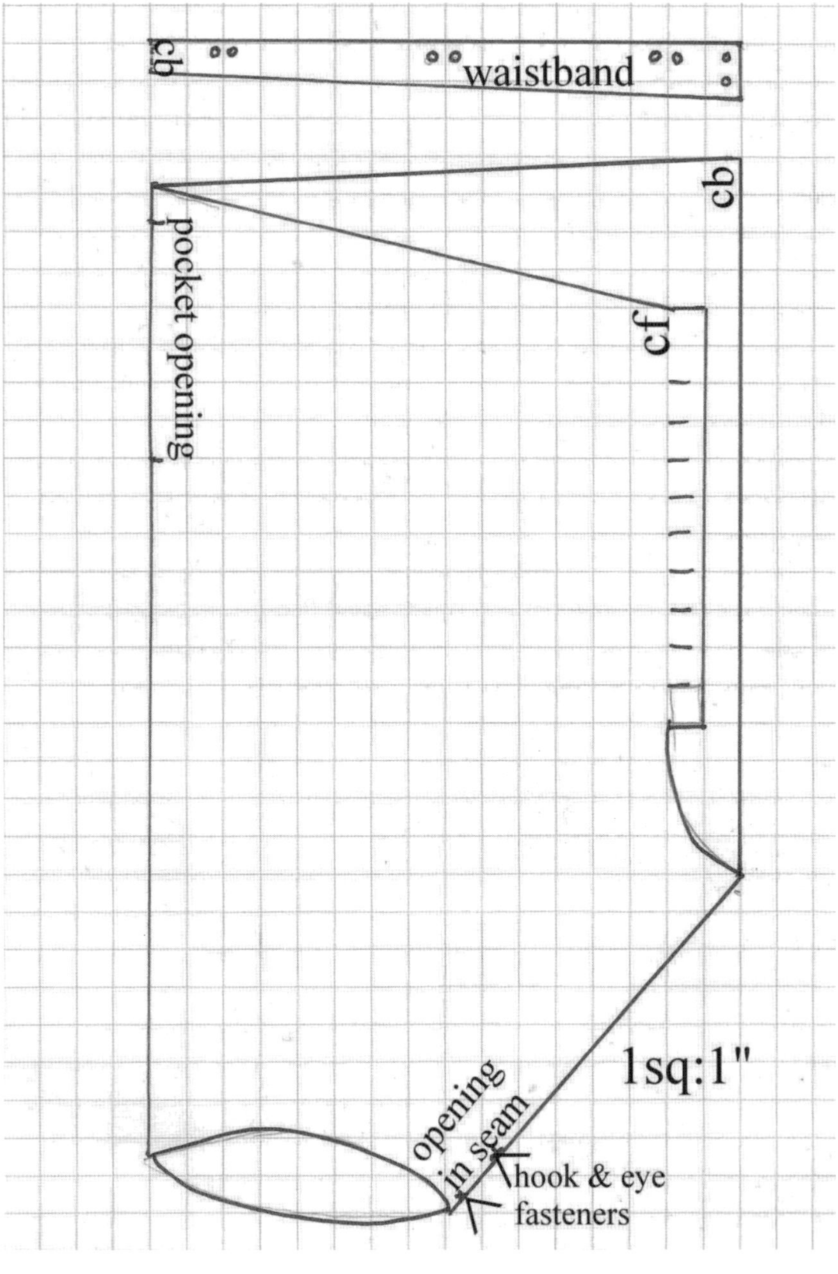

cb

waistband

cb

pocket opening

cf

opening in seam

hook & eye fasteners

1 sq:1"

The lining, interlining and outer pieces are all cut to the same pattern. The opening fastened with hooks and eyes is on the inside seam of the leg.

The front of the leg is longer at the knee than the back.

Venetians 1580's to 1610's

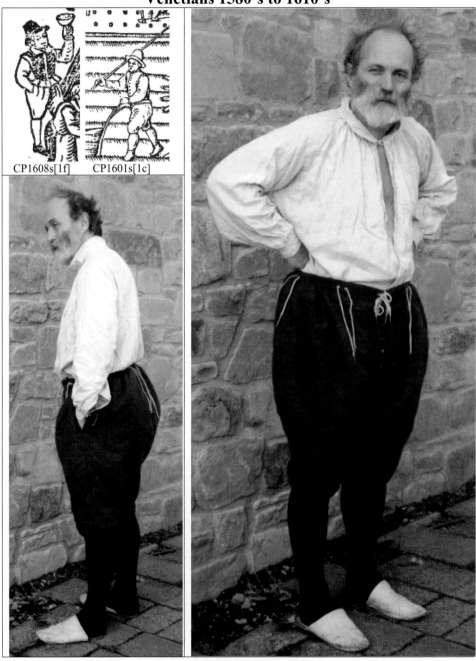

CP1608s[1f]   CP1601s[1c]

Venetians with points in undyed russet lined with linen and interlined with cotton.

Pockets are set into the side seams.

Above the Knee Breeches 1610's to early 1630's

CP1626s[1a]

Above the knee breeches with hooks, in undyed gray russet lined with linen, with a stout canvas interliner on the bands. Pockets are set into the side seams.

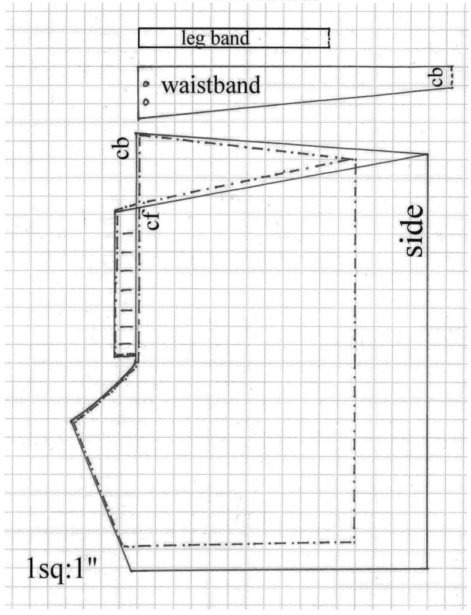

The dot-dash line is the pattern for the linen liner.

The waist and leg bands have a linen liner and canvas interliner to the same pattern as the outer.

Baggy Breeches Pattern

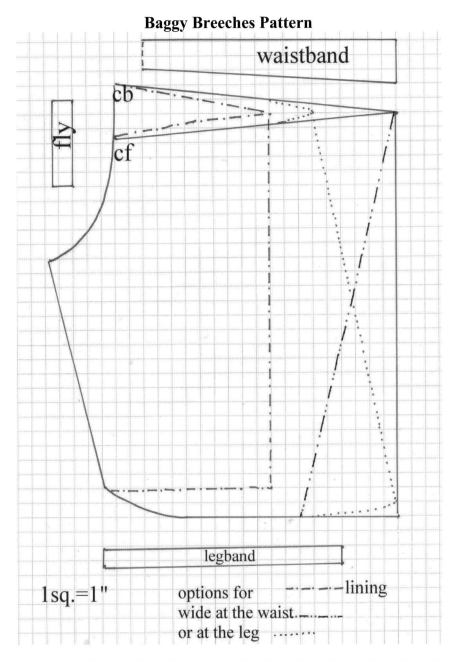

waistband

fly

cb

cf

legband

1 sq.=1"

options for
wide at the waist
or at the leg

lining

Cut a canvas interliner for the waistband, cut a linen liner for each part. The waistband and leg bands are made up and the main part gathered at waist and knee with cartridge pleating before being sewn to the bands.

Variants: there are various cuts; tapering to knee, big mid thigh and big at the knee. Alternative lengths of liner, some shorter than the outer produce variations in the style.

Baggy Breeches 1610's-1650's

When inserting lining adjust the leg length for the desired bagginess

Grey russet with linen liner, points and pockets. There are many variations on this form, some are baggy all the way down the leg [shown] some baggier at the waist, some at the knee and some in the middle.

Simple or Tapering Breeches 1610's to 1650's

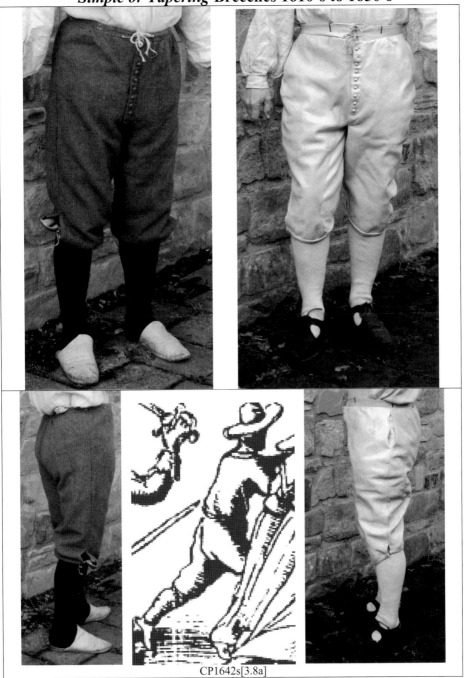

CP1642s[3.8a]

Tapering Breeches with hooks, in Gray russet and in oiled deerskin, both lined with linen, with a stout canvas interliner on the bands. Pockets are set into the side seams.

Tapering Breeches Patterns

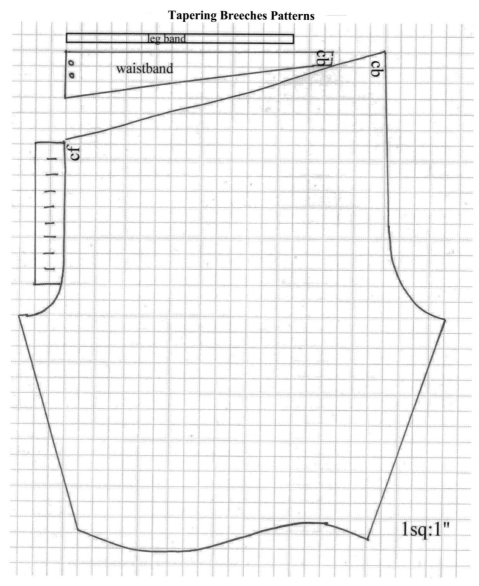

leg band

waistband

cb

cb

cf

1sq:1"

In addition cut stout canvas interliners for the waistband and leg bands.

The fly may be cut in with the main panel or separate.

Chapter 5
Male Waistcoats and Pettycoats[58]

Male petticoats occur up to 1599 and male waistcoats after that date. They are made from similar fabrics in similar colours and probably performed similar functions.

Male Pettycoats				Male Waistcoats		
Colour	Number	%	Notes	Number	%	Notes
White	5	83%	2 Cloth, 2 Russet, 1 Cotton	1	33%	Cotton
Red	1	17%		1	33%	
Green				1	33%	Cotton
Materials						
Russet	5	38%				
Cotton	3	21%		2	50%	
Cloth	2	14%		1 coarse	25%	
Canvas	1	7%				
Frizado	1?	7%				
Huss?	1	7%				
Knit	1	7%		1	25%	

They are simple single skin garments, worn over the shirt but under the doublet and tucked into the breeches, for additional warmth in cold weather. While there is evidence that some were sleeved in other cases there seems insufficient fabric and like a young child's knitted waistcoat in the Museum of London some are probably sleeveless.

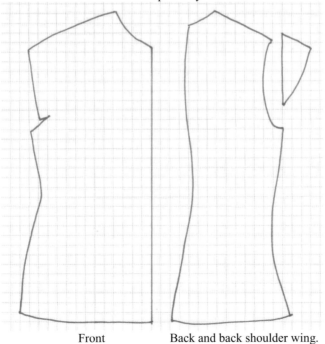

Front   Back and back shoulder wing.

---

[58] See Volume 11

Sleeveless Male Waistcoat 1600-1660

Childs knitted waistcoat

Sleeveless waistcoat in woad and weld dyed green cotton with red madder dyed wool tape woven with a simple heddle loom. For economy of fabric cutting the front shoulder wing is cut with the main panel and the rear shoulder wing is cut separately.

Green waistcoats with red tape were sent from England to workmen servants in Massachusetts in 1629.

Sleeved Male Waistcoat 1600-1660

Edmund Parker in 1593 wearing, beneath a piped leather doublet but over his shirt, a red sleeved garment showing at collar and cuffs. This may be a waistcoat with a collar. Parker himself is not common.

Full sleeved waistcoat in Madder dyed Red Cotton.

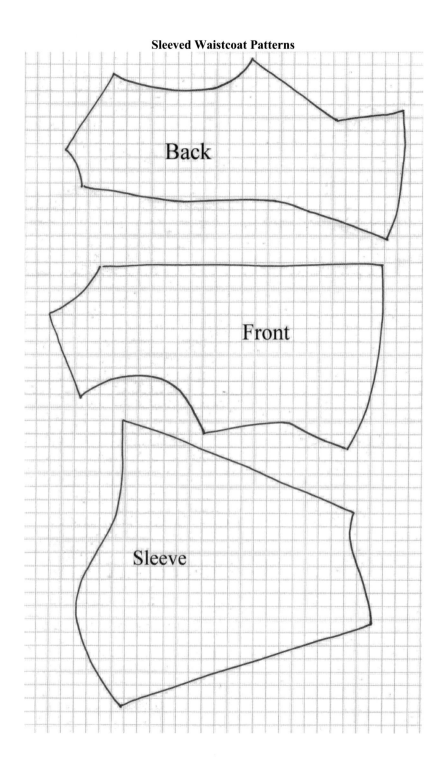

Shirts

Four main materials were mentioned for shirts; Canvas [54%], Lockram [24%], Flax [14%] and Holland [7%]. It is not unusual for an individual to have both canvas and lockram shirts, both made from hemp but of different qualities. The courser canvas shirts may be workday while the lockram may be holiday wear. Many shirts were of bleached materials while others were "brown" unbleached or boiled linens.

Shirt Patterns

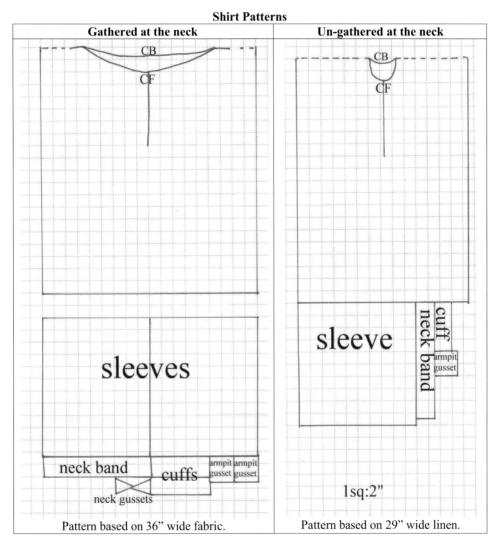

Gathered at the neck	Un-gathered at the neck
Pattern based on 36" wide fabric.	Pattern based on 29" wide linen.

A typical shirt required about 120 inches of linen around 27" to 36" wide.

Male Shirts: Gathered and Ungathered at the Neck

Gathered at the Neck.	Ungathered at the Neck.

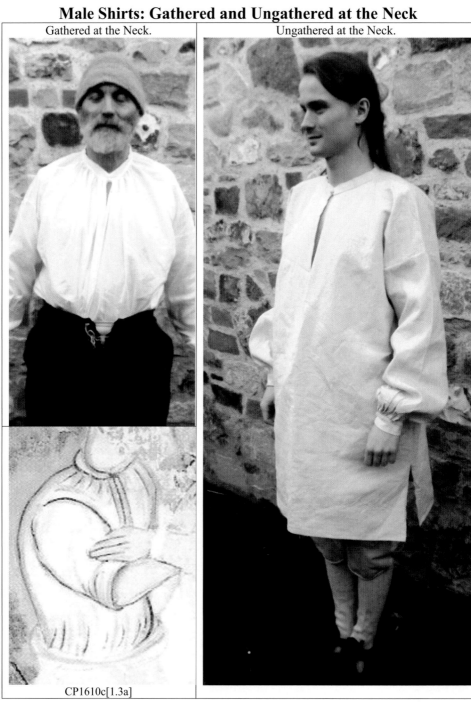

CP1610c[1.3a]

Collars, Cuffs and Ruffs

Men wore a variety of Collars, Ruffs and Hand Ruffs around the neck and wrists. Hand ruffs are very rarely shown and only on men who are also wearing ruffs [See page 106].

Plain Band	Flat Fronted Collar
Laced Darted Falling Band	Plain Darted Falling Band

Ruffs were considered higher status that bands. Unset ruffs or frills are seen on common men from the 1550's to at least the 1580's, more formal starched and set ruffs from at least the 1590's to the 1640's.

Male Ruffs and Ruff Cuffs appear similar to women's[59].

Unset Ruff or Frill

Starched and Set Ruff

---

[59] See pages 153 and 155 for ruff construction details.

Band Patterns[60]

Plain Band [1 square = 1 inch]
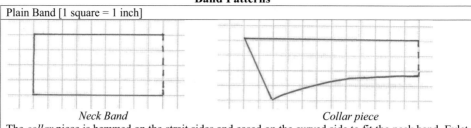

Neck Band   *Collar piece*

The *collar* piece is hemmed on the strait sides and eased on the curved side to fit the neck band. Eylet holes at the front edges allow for band strings to tie the ends together.

Plain Darted Falling Band	*Flat Fronted* Collar
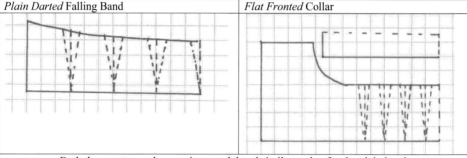	

Both these patterns also require a neck band similar to that for the plain band.

Men who have stripped down to their shirts for heavy work do not have bands but many common men mention workday bands implying also holiday bands, probably in differing qualities of linen. Bands were more visible than shirts and were often of a finer fabric. Holland seems the norm. Cambric and Lawn appear in some inventories but were forbidden to London Apprentices in 1611. In 1630 in New England "the poorer sort" used "blew Callico" handkerchiefs as bands in the summer. This is possibly what is shown on this English sailor in the tropics:	 CP1642s[2]

Male Aprons[61]

 CP1652s[1.1a] Butchers Boy	Men only wear aprons for work, usually of linen, sometimes dyed blue, but some trades using sharp knives such as cobblers and fish gutters used leather. Men's aprons never extend far below the knee and are often much shorter with only around 9 inches of drop. Almost all appear to be simple rectangles of cloth in some cases only tucked into a belt particularly with tapsters. Shoemakers and cobblers aprons may have a "bib" covering the chest.	 CP1641s[9b] Brewer

---

[60] See Volume 17. There are a number of other variations of collars.
[61] See Volume 17

Chapter 6

Overgarments

Men's Jerkins[62]

Jerkins were probably sleeveless, although in a number of cases sleeves, probably detachable and sometimes specified as leather, are mentioned. Jerkins could be lined with cotton or bays and occasionally cut or even trimmed with fur or lace. Jerkins were recorded having between 13 and 24 metal buttons while London Apprentices were permitted to have silk buttons and buttonholes on their jerkins in 1611.

Jerkin Colours			
Black	13	42%	4 frieze, 2 leather, 1 sealskin, 1 fustian.
White	4	13%	All Frieze
Gray	3	10%	1 Frieze
Blue	3	10%	2 blue, 1 sky
Green	2	6%	1 French Green
Red	1	3%	
Tawney	1	3%	
Violet	1	3%	
Marbled	1	3%	
Motley	2	6%	

Few jerkins specify a colour and of those that do two thirds are black, grey or white, all of which might be natural undyed colours, except for those of fustian or leather. Over 90% of jerkins are russet, frieze or leather and as these are thought to be normally undyed materials it is probable that most common peoples Jerkins were undyed.

Jerkin Materials	Number	%		Leather Details	Number	Percentage of specified leathers
Leather	55	41%		**Buff**	10	36%
Frieze	48	36%		**Buck skin**	5	18%
Russet	21	16%		**Doe skin**	1	4%
Cloth	7	5%		**Sealskin**	2	7%
Selfgrow	1	1%		**Sheep**	1	4%
Silk	1	1%		**Spanish**	6	21%
Canvas	1	1%		**Spruce**	3	11%
Fustian	1	1%		**Unspecified**	27	-
				Jerkins could be of either tanned or tawed leather		

Jerkin Styles

Jerkins came in a wide variety of styles although the variation seems to be with function rather than changing fashions over time. Thick leather jerkins with large tabs seem to be used for protection while working, especially by draymen [Type1]. Frieze and russet jerkins were probably worn mainly for warmth and had gathered skirts [Type 2]. Jerkin Doublets may have been similar to the doublet pattern but without the sleeves and the internal band for points or eyes [Type 3].

Another variation [right] on some type 2 and 3 jerkins was to have a truncated arm only 4 or 5 inches long.

CP1592s[1.1] labourer

---

[62] See Volume 12

Jerkins

Both these Type 3 Jerkins were cut to the flange doublet pattern omitting the sleeves

Sealskin jerkin	Oiled deerskin leather jerkin

Type 1 Jerkins of Vegetable Tanned Leather

The counterfet Cranke
Nicolas Geninges.

CP1592nl[1a]

CP1636s[2a]

98

Type 2 Jerkins 1560's to 1650's

Jerkin with gathered skirts in gray russet lined with gray cotton and pewter buttons.
Many type 2 jerkins were probably made of frieze.

Type 2 Jerkin Pattern

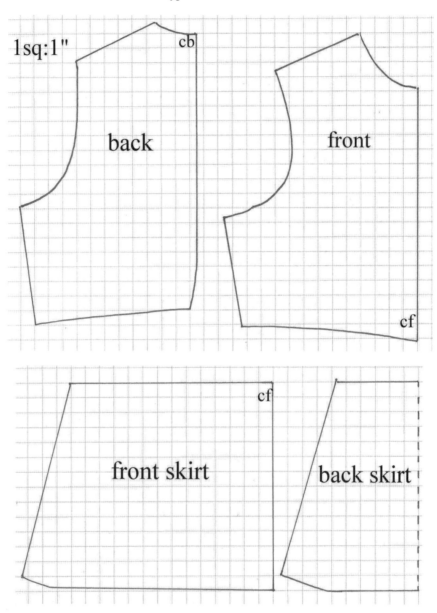

1sq:1"

cb

back

front

cf

front skirt

cf

back skirt

The skirt is composed of 4 panels which are gathered onto the waist of the upper part. Shoulder wings and collar are optional. Some illustrations thought to be the type 2 jerkins may be sleeved coats of similar design [See the next section on coats for sleeve patterns].

This reproduction is closed down the front with 17 pewter button at regular intervals. The shanks of the buttons go through the fabric are strung on a linen lace on the inside which prevents then coming out. They are not sewn on.

Mandillions[63]

A mandillion was similar to a jerkin but with useless vestigial sleeves hanging down the back. Mandillions are mainly institutional outer garments issued to soldiers and colonists to America. Red, blue and green mandillions are recorded for Elizabethan soldiers and most were probably coloured. Most seem to have been woollen but a canvas one owned by a labourer is recorded. Mandillions for American colonists in 1629 were to have small hooks and eyes and mandillions do not appear to use buttons on the front closure. These were also lined with white cotton.

Like Jerkins mandillions came in a variety of styles, some of a short doublet body style, tabbed flanged or scalloped [bottom right pattern], others extended in one piece to the lower thigh [top right].

CP1635sr[3c]

John Smith Virginian Mandillion Pattern

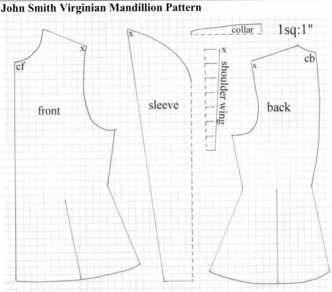

The sleeve is left open along the top seam. The back of the sleeve is attached to the back of the arm hole. The front of the sleeve is attached only at the top shoulder marked x so that the wearer's arm may come through the arm hole in front of the whole sleeve.

Running Servant [below left] *Scalloped Tab* **Mandillion Pattern**

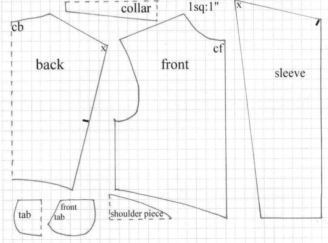

This pattern requires 9 scalloped tabs. The 2 of these at the front have a slightly different shape [front tab on pattern.]. The sleeve part attaches only to the back of the arm hole and has no front.

---

[63] See Volume 12

Mandillions

Long Mandillion		
		Long Mandillion in White kersey lined with plunket coloured cotton dyed with woad and weld. The edges are bound with unbleached linen cut on the bias. secured down the front with hooks and eyes. Based on a Mandillion illustrated on Captain Smith in Virginia in 1609: 

Short Mandillion with Scalloped Tabs		
		Short mandillion with scalloped tabs in woad dyed russet weight fabric lined with white baize, secured down the front with hooks and eyes.  Variant with square tabs

Male Cassocks[64] 1560's to 1610's

Thomas Trevelion pre 1608

Right: Soldier's cassock in woad dyed russet weight wool fully lined with weld dyed cotton.
Left: Coarse canvas sailor's cassock bound with linen tape.

---

[64] See Volume 13

Male Cassocks

Cassocks are mainly worn by soldiers and sailors. Sailor's cassocks may have commonly been made of canvas although some are recorded of cotton, frieze, white blanket and wadmoll.

While it was hoped to trade blue, red, yellow and green cotton cassocks to Indians in Newfoundland the rare civilian cassocks recorded in England were with the exception on one blue cassock either black or white and as most were of frieze probably also natural browns and greys. Nearly half the civilian cassocks with any details recorded were owned by brewers including canvas cassocks and, in the 1550's and 1560's, cassocks faced with fox or rabbit.

The soldiers in the Lant Roll [right] are described as wearing Cassockins. These are baggy, hip length garments which do not open down the front but may have slits at the side and are similar to garments shown on some sailors.

Military cassocks came in a wide range of colours and could be made of broadcloth or frieze. Some were lined in the body with cotton. By the late 1620's a new type of military cassock may have been introduced with 120-180 buttons but the only definite issue was to a general's 30 man guard who may have been above common status.

Cassock Pattern

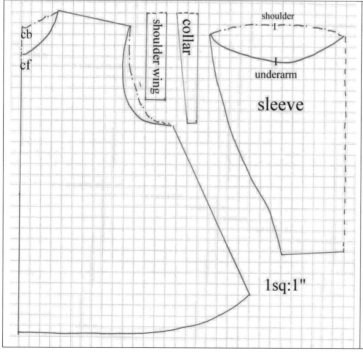

The dot-dash line is the line of the back piece of the cassock. Cut two fronts and two backs.

The seam on the sleeve lines up with half way down the back of the armhole.

The front pieces are sewn together leaving the top 6 inches open.

Coats[65]

Coats may sometimes be used at the period as a catchall term encompassing a range of outer garments such as cassocks, jerkins and mandillions. This might explain occasional references to coats without sleeves. It is thought that men's coats at the period were sleeved woollen garments worn for warmth and protection from the elements.

Coat Colours

While most coats were probably natural undyed greys, browns, whites and blacks many coats were clearly dyed, especially in blue. There is an association in literature between blue coats and servants but 88% of the blue coats in the mortext were not owned by servants. Blue was the most colourfast common man's dye, important when working outdoors.

Coat Colours			Percentage of each occupation in that colour				
Colour	Total	%	Labourers	Husband	Yeoman	Artizans	Servants
Black	56	44%	14%	55%	43%	50%	14%
White	8	6%	14%	3%	11%	-	14%
Blue	34	27%	50%	16%	26%	22%	57%
Tawney	7	5%	7%	10%	6%	3%	-
Green	5	4%	-	6%	6%	3%	-
Red	5	4%	7%	-	-	8%	14%
Violet	3	2%	-	3%	-	5%	-
Grey	1	1%	-	3%	-	-	-
Puke	1	1%	-	-	-	3%	-
Pink	1	1%	-	-	3%	-	-
Marble	6	5%	-	3%	6%	8%	-
Medley	1	1%	7%	-	-	-	-
	128		14	31	35	40	7

Material

	Number	%	Agricultural	Artizan	Servants
Frieze	97	72%	51	43	3
Russet	22	16%	16	6	-
Broadcloth/cloth	5	4%	1	2	1
Frizado	2	1%	1	1	-
Kendal	1	1%	1	-	-
Bays	1	1%	-	1	-
Worsted	1	1%			
Leather	3	2%	2	1	-
Buff	1	1%			
Canvas	1	1%		1	
	134				

The vast majority of coats were of thick warm frieze with a significant number in russet. Some of the less common materials such as canvas and leather may be a result of the catchall nature of the word. Some coats are referred to as livery coats. There is no evidence that this was a particular design or colour [one man had 2 white, one blue and one plunket livery coats] but were probably given as part of a livery agreement and may have had a badge on the sleeve. Some livery coats were supplied to town officials. Soldier's coats in the English Civil War weighed around 3lb.

---

[65] See Volume 13

Loose Coat with 4 Panel Straight Skirt 1560's to 1650's

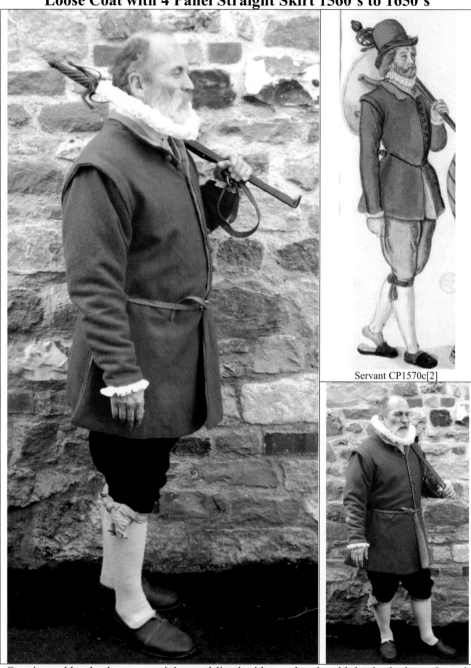

Servant CP1570c[2]

Coat in madder dyed, russet weight wool lined with woad and weld dyed, plunket coloured cotton and cloth buttons. The skirt has separate panels below the waist with the join obscured by the leather girdle. This form can be found throughout the period although the 1570 picture above is somewhat more fitted than some other images.

Coats with No Waist Join 1600-1640's [Possibly 1590's to 1650's]

Coat with shoulder rolls	Coats without shoulder rolls.

Natural black russet lined with madder dyed cotton.

Unlined russet coat without shoulder rolls

Russet weight fabric 1640's soldiers coat with shoulder rolls, dyed green with weld and woad with a yellow cotton liner [the colours given for Col. John Hamden's regiment of foot].

Loose Coat with 4 Panel Straight Skirt Pattern

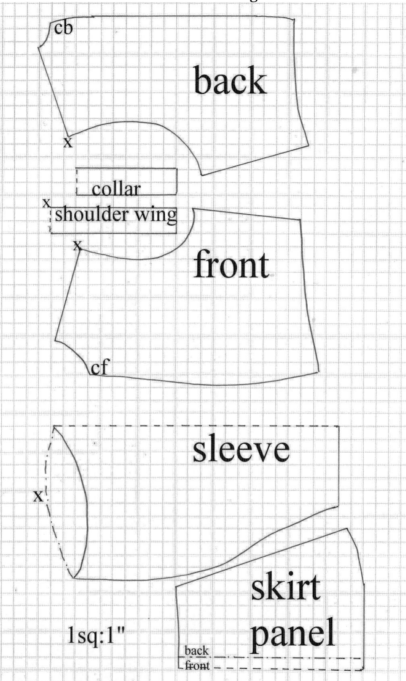

All the points marked x are touching. The sleeve seam goes at the back. The two front skirt panels are slightly larger than the back two.

Coats with No Waist Join Patterns

The pattern below was used for the green and yellow soldiers coat on page 107. The Black and red coat on that page is the same coat without the shoulder rolls. This is a very economic pattern with virtually no waste or curved lines. The buttons are made from what little scrap there is. This pattern fits man 5'6" tall.

Detail on right shows the v of the coat body inset into the sleeve.

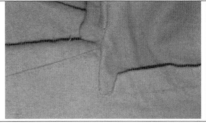

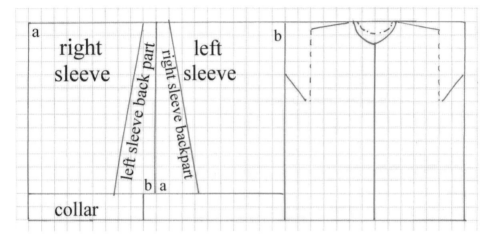

The pattern below is for a larger flared version of the coat as used on the unlined grey coat on page 107. It can optionally have shoulder wings. Fits a man 6' 2" tall.

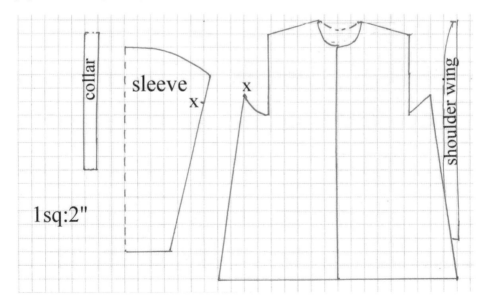

109

Long Coats
Early style: 1590's-1610's. Late style: late 1640's?-1650's

Undyed frieze coat lined with white cotton, pinned at the chest and worn with a linen band. The early long coats are sometimes shown with 2 pins and sometimes shoulder rolls, the later style may have broader, slightly longer sleeves allowing large turnbacks.

Riding Coat: 1620's -1640's

These were loose coats often of cotton worn over other clothes to protect them from mud while riding.

The reconstruction shows an unlined natural grey cotton riding coat. The buttons only extend to the waist. Period images do not show the front and the buttons may have extended to the bottom edge.

Short Coat 1650's

Short coat in gray russet with white baize lining and cloth buttons. This is shown worn with a darted collar beneath which is a conjectured small collar.

Long Coat Pattern	**Riding Coat Pattern**
back front sleeve 1 sq:1"	collar back front sleeve 1 sq:1" additional back panel
A narrow collar can be added similar to the riding coat pattern [top right].	The additional back panel can be cut to a fold or added to the width of the back panel if the fabric is wide enough.

Short Coat Pattern

1sq:1"

X

sleeve

X

collar

X

front

X

back

The sleeve seam goes at the back. Points marked x touch. With all three patterns coth buttons can be made from the offcuts.

Male Gowns

A man's gown was a garment covering at least the upper body, open and not fastened down the front. There was a wide range of gown colours although black predominates, no doubt assisted by the giving of black mourning gowns to the poor. Gowns are generally impractical for physical work and are more colourful than many common men's garments

Gown Colours	Number	%	Notes
Black	9	45%	
Blue	3	15%	1 blue, 1 sky coloured
Murrey	2	10%	
Puke	2	10%	
Red	1	5%	
Scarlet	1	5%	Possibly town livery: alderman
Green	1	5%	
Gray	1	5%	

74% of gowns were made of frieze or russet, over three quarters of these of the thicker winter weight frieze. The prime function of almost all gowns appears to have been warmth.

Gown Fabrics	Number	%	Notes
Frieze and Rug	27	63%	2 donations to the poor, 2 frieze mantle, 1 rag/rug
Russet	8	19%	1 donation to the poor
Broadcloth	2	5%	1 donation to the poor
Cloth	2	5%	1 donation to the poor
Stuff	2	5%	
Grograin	1	2%	
Wadmoll	1	2%	Donation to poor

This emphasis on warmth continues with the lining, where specified they are either another layer of woollen cloth, such as bays or cotton, or fur:

Gown Linings	Number	Notes
Conie	1	All faced with fur or furred
Lamb	1	
White bays	2	
Cotton	1	

The cuffs of some gowns could be decoratively faced with fur or satin or even furred down the front edge.

Faced with	Number	Furred with	Number
Satin	1	Fox	2
Bridge [Bruges satin]	1	Frycholle [Polecat]	1
Russels	1		
Fur	1		
Budge [lamb]	3		
Fox	2		
Coney	1		
Foynes [beech marten]	1		
Black Lamb	1		

Early Full Sleeved Gown 1560's to 1620's?

The Early Full Sleeved Gown in gray frieze lined with white baize and furred with red fox.

Half Split Sleeved Gown 1560's to 1650's

Night Watchman and Dog

CP1609nl[1]

Split sleeved gown in brown russet fabric lined with grey cotton.

Pattern for *half split sleeved* gown

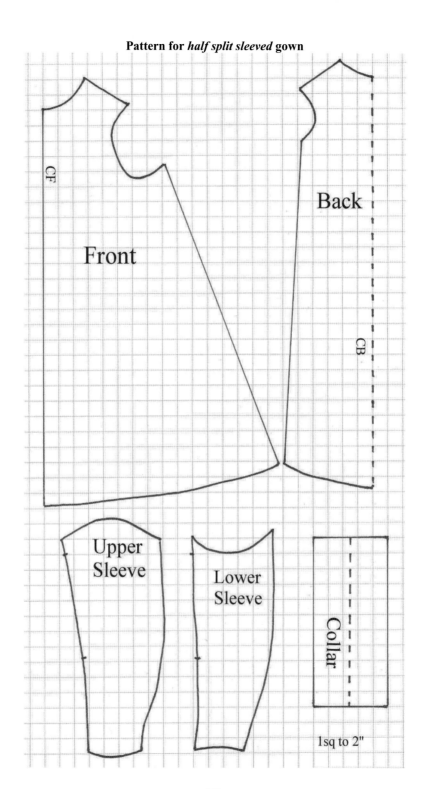

CF

Back

Front

CB

Upper
Sleeve

Lower
Sleeve

Collar

1sq to 2"

Pattern for *Early Full Sleeved* Gown

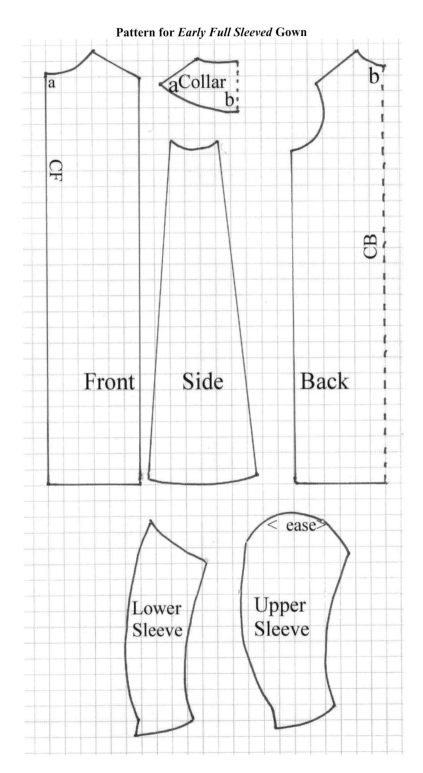

Lant Roll Mourning Gown

CP1587s[1.1]

Lant Roll Mourning Gown Pattern

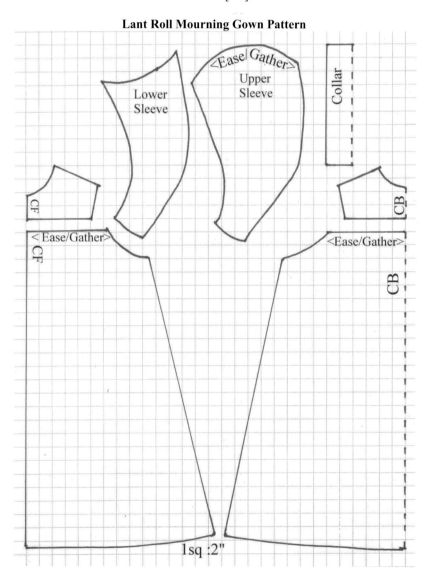

Male Frock

CP1605s[1b]
London Porter after 1605

From the limited evidence Frocks seem to be made from canvas or linen and to be white, possibly bleached by repeated washing as their function is to cover the rest of the clothing from dirt and grime for people largely of the labouring class. Many seem not to have a front opening although some garments of similar shape do open. Whether all these are frocks is unclear.

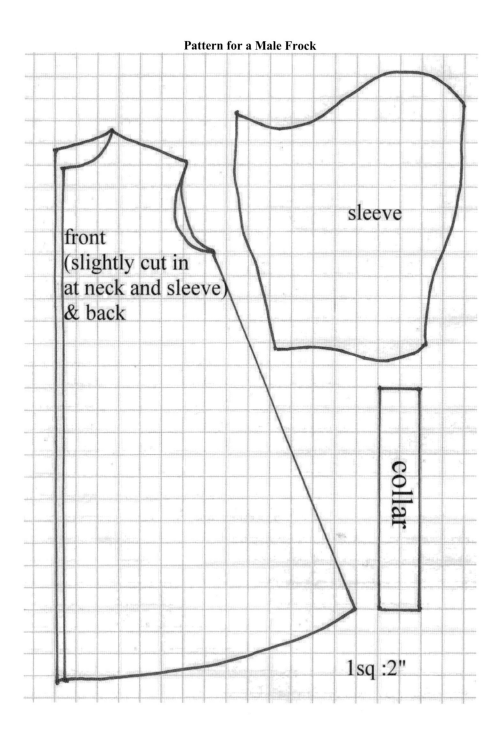

sleeve

front
(slightly cut in
at neck and sleeve)
& back

collar

1sq :2"

Male Cloak

Most cloaks are made of the medium weight woolen fabric russet although many are coloured. They are probably more for protection from rain and in some cases for display than for warmth. The cloaks shown on common men usually extend down to the mid thigh but a second category, servant's livery cloaks and mourning cloaks, both very occasionally provided for common men by the rich, appear to be full length. Mourning cloaks appear undecorated, and partly explain the large number of black cloaks, but at least some livery cloaks were decorated with lace and a few richer common men had cloaks faced with silk or furred.

Colour

	Number	%	Notes
Black	20	54%	
Blue	7	19%	4 blue, 2 sky colour, 1 watchet.
Green	4	11%	2 green, 2 greenish.
Gray	2	5%	Both old
Sheep's russet	1	3%	
Puke	1	3%	
Tawney	1	3%	
Violet	1	3%	

Material

Fabric	Number	% of specified
Russet	16	94%
Frizado	1	6%
Unspecified cloth	4	

Lining

Cloaks seem to be commonly lined, most usually with bays, in one case the bays is specified as white as is the only frieze lining.

Lining Materials	Number	%
Bays	5	83%
White Frieze	1	17%

Most cloaks appear to be closed at the throat with a large button or clasp although they are usually shown worn open at the neck.

Some cloaks had sleeves and buttons and these may have been for riding

Left: CP1605s[1c] London Porter best dress

Right: CP1605c[1l] London street trader buying old gold or silver.

Mourning Cloak 1580's

Broadcloth mourning cloak lined with a strip of black silk along the front edge and collar. Livery cloaks could be more ornamental with buttons and lace.

This reproduction is based on the cloaks at the funeral of Sir Phillip Sydney in 1586 but may be more widely applicable.

Mid Length Cloak 1600-1660

And to our Hall,thus we goe all.

London Porter CP1605s[1c]

Mid length cloak in grey russet lined with white baize.

While images can be found for this type of cloak through the first 6 decades of the 17th century it may also be appropriate for the cloaks in inventories in the Elizabethan period when images are absent from the record.

Pattern for a Mid Length Russet Cloak

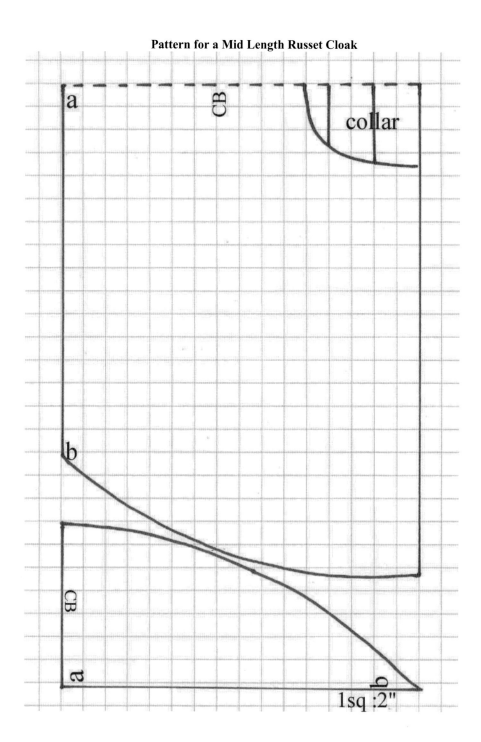

a

CB

collar

b

CB

a

b

1sq :2"

124

Chapter 7

Women's Garments with Overbodies

Women's clothing falls into three types, firstly items worn with an overbody to support the bust, typically including a skirt, secondly looser outer garments worn for warmth but not support and thirdly linens[66].

Women's Pettycoats

The principal garment for a woman was the petticoat, often with a permanently attached overbody. This performs the same function as the male doublet and breeches providing leg covering and an upper garment tailored close to the body. Beneath it lay the linen smock and over it the outer warm woollen layers.

Petticoats were made from 3-4 square yards of material, normally russet.

Materials used for Petticoats

Russet	55	74%	
Frizado	4	5%	1 red
Cotton	4	5%	2 red, 2 white
Flannel	3	4%	
Cloth	2	3%	
Rugg	1	1%	1 white
Worsted	1	1%	
Searge	1	1%	
Selfgrow	1	1%	
Linsey Woolsey	1	1%	Uncertain status
Phillip and Cheyney	1	1%	
	74		

The white, sheeps colour and possibly some of the black petticoats would have been undyed. Apart from the two blue petticoats all the coloured petticoats are red or the related stammel.

Colours	number		
Red	81	76%	
Stammell	7	7%	
White	12	11%	
Black	3	3%	
Blue	2	2%	
Sheeps Colour	1	1%	Plus 55 russet
	106		

Petticoat Styles

By the 1590's illustrations, such as those of London markets, show a different body profile with very full, gathered pettycoats. In contrast early Elizabethan petticoats [pre 1580's] were shown not gathered at the waist [see page 146].

---

[66] See Volumes 21, 22 and 23 respectively for details.

Working Women in Petticoat and Bodice

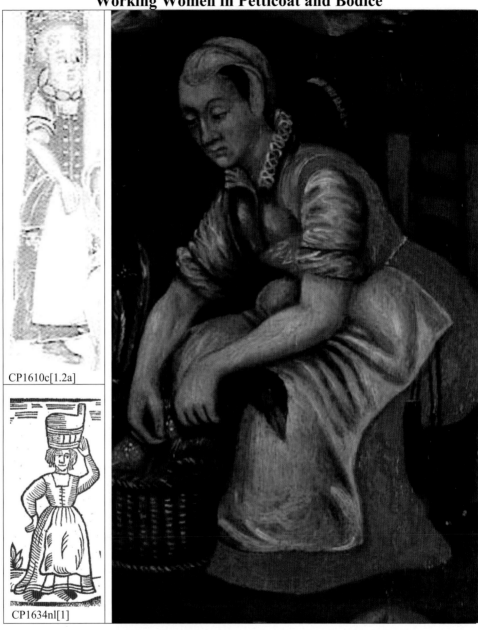

CP1610c[1.2a]

CP1634nl[1]

The two images in red are probably of women who are household heads while the woodcut is of a milk maid, typically a young servant. The two matrons have their sleeves rolled up to the upper arm for messy work but both have ruffs on their smocks.

Gathered Petticoats 1580's to 1650's

Madder dyed red russet weight petticoats with either a similar madder or weld dyed overbody or an unbleached canvas overbody. On the weld overbody the edges are turned in while the madder and canvas overbodies have tape bound edges.

Petticoat Patterns

Later Gathered Petticoat

This garment requires 3 rectangles of cloth. To determine the length of fabric required for a petticoat, measure from waist to ankle and add at least 1" hem allowance plus 1" top turn over. This usually gives a total length of between 36"- 48". For fabric 30-36" wide use 3 drops to give adequate width for the stride.

Gather the top of the fabric with cartridge pleats onto a linen tape (10mm - 13mm wide is best) long enough to go around the waist and with enough left to tie in a bow. The petticoat is more tightly gathered if it is for a small waist. Leave a flat panel at the front, as shown below. In the middle at the front cut and hem a small slit to enable the petticoat to slip over the hips. This will be covered by the wearer's apron or kirtle.

 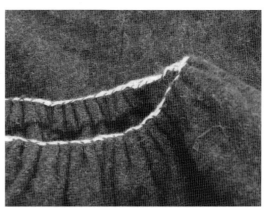

Cartridge pleating onto the tape

If sewing the petticoat to the upper body, sew the petticoat tape onto the outside of the lower edge of the overbody for the length of the pleats. The flat front may have been left un-sewn and thus able to be tucked under the front of the bodies as below or it could have been sewn down.

Ungathered Petticoat Pattern

Early Elizabethan petticoats such as the 1570 English Villager[67] do not appear from the illustrations to be significantly gathered at the waist. The panels are sewn onto the bottom of the overbody. The front slit is concealed by the kirtle or apron.

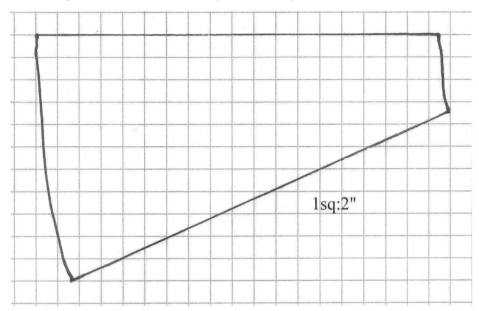

1sq:2"

This panel is symmetrical. Depending on the width of the fabric it can be cut with the centre line of the panel along the grain of the fabric in which case the choice is open as to whether the front of the garment is a panel or a seam. Alternatively as shown above the panel can be cut with one edge aligned with the grain in which case this becomes the centre front or centre back seam. For slightly more fullness the back panels can be larger and slightly gathered.

This ungathered petticoat pattern can used for a petticoat of the early Elizabethan period and possibly also to go under a kirtle later on.

Binding on the bottom edge of this or the other petticoat pattern will protect the main fabric from wear and is probably indicated in a number of the woodcuts. Worn biding can be easily replaced as required.

Decoration
Most petticoats appear to have been undecorated but there are rare references to coloured lace, probably lines of tape rather than frilly lace, applied in horizontal bands near the bottom [See the milk maid above]. References to fringe are even rarer and when present this was probably along the bottom edge of the petticoat.

---

[67] CP1570c[1]

Ungathered Petticoat: up to 1580's

A russet petticoat with the canvas overbody bound along the edge with white linen tape. This would have been worn with either an apron or, possibly for the better off common women on more formal occasions, a kirtle to cover the front slit in the petticoat.

Overbodies

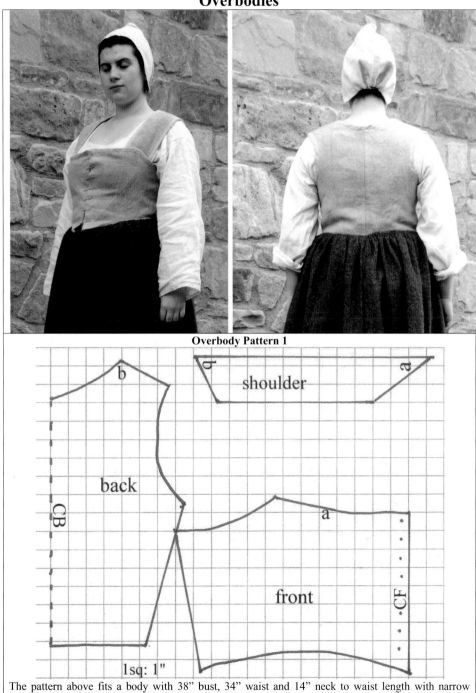

Overbody Pattern 1

b

shoulder

a

back

CB

a

front

CF

1 sq: 1"

The pattern above fits a body with 38" bust, 34" waist and 14" neck to waist length with narrow shoulders, as shown above.

Fitting Overbody Patterns

An overbody is a closely fitting garment and needs to be made to the body shape rather than just bust and waist measurements. It is the most closely fitting garment a woman wears.

Producing an Overbody Toile[68]

The first diagram contains the basic shapes for a toile for an overbody from which, with adjustments, an overbody pattern can be made to fit any bodily shape. Two copies of each piece need to be made, one for the left and one for right hand sides of the overbody. Cut these pieces out, pin or tack them together, try them on and then adjust until the toile is a close fit. This is far easier with a friend.

Overbody Toile Pattern

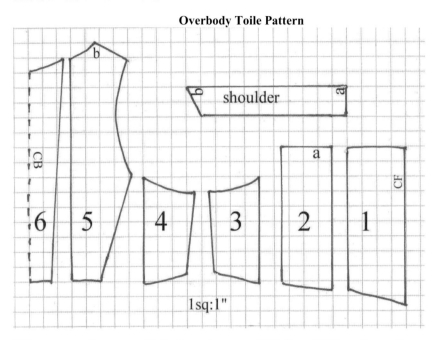

With no seam allowance added this pattern is suitable for a 36" bust. By adding a generous seam allowance up to a 44" bust can be accommodated.

Once the toile fits, sew the panels together. From this shape a pattern can be cut with fewer seams. The following examples have a single back panel and two front panels lacing up the front. The seams are towards the back, between panels 4 and 5. The size and number of panels can be adjusted to suit fabric pieces for efficiency.

---

[68] A toile is a pattern made out of cheap light fabric which can be easily adjusted to make a good fit before cutting out the real material.

Overbody Pattern 2

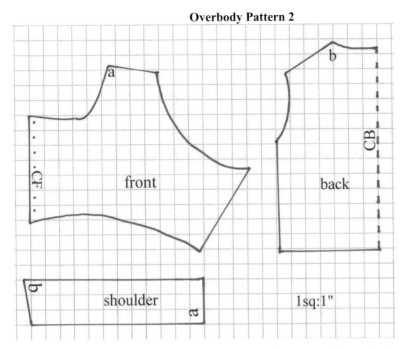

The pattern above fits a body with 46" bust, 40" waist, 16" neck to waist length with broad shoulders. This is the pattern used for the overbody on page 127 [right] which has a madder russet weight outer layer and is linen lined with a buckram interliner.

In 1611 it was decreed that "no maidservant or womanservant whatsoever dwelling or shall hereafter dwell within the city of London or the liberties thereof, which shall take any wages... [shall] wear ... any "fardingale" at all, either little or great, nor any body or sleeves of wyer whalebones or with other stiffening, save canvas or buckram only,".

Experimental reconstructions show that it is far more comfortable for a working woman to have no ridged stiffening in the body. Not only does stiffening make bending less comfortable but rigid stiffening will wear through the outerbody. Such considerations were not applicable to the great and the good wearing their finest clothes in portraits who sailed upright across rooms with servants to pick up anything they dropped. Their clothing is not relevant to working women cooking on fires on the floor, picking up children or weeding the garden.

Straight Laced
Overbodies were laced up the front. This lace was often shown running zig-zaged or diagonaly. The term straight laced is often misunderstood to mean laced straight across when it actually meant tightly laced in the sense of a constricted maritime straight or being in straightened circumstances.

Maid with Melons

CP1620c[1] [Tate Gallery]

CP1620c[2] Note the flap across the front of the overbody.

Details of pined detachable sleves

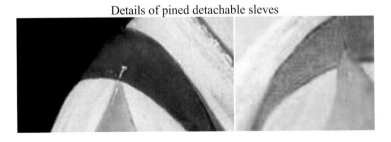

Detachable sleeves

On the previous pages two contemporary English paintings circa 1620 from a series by Nathaniel Bacon show maids wearing yellow three quarter length sleeves. They may well be the same sleeves used in both paintings. The sleeves are attached by pins at the shoulder to the straps of the overbodies.

Women's Sleeves Materials and Colours

Knitted sleeves form nearly half of those mentioned and in two cases the bequeathed sleeves were the woman's best implying she had multiple knitted sleeves.

Material	Certainly common status	Uncertain status	Total
Knit	1	2 [best]	3
Chamlet	1		1
Lockram		1	1
Linen		1	1
Russet		1	1
Colour			
White	1		

A variety of sleeve styles are recorded although the status of the owners is uncertain. A "long" sleeve may cover the arm from wrist to shoulder, a "hand sleeve" may a sleeve reaching down to the hand and thus the same as a long sleeve. "Fore sleeve" may be a foreshortened sleeve, not reaching beyond the middle of the fore arm and only just meeting the shoulder, as with Bacons maids.

Stomachers

Stomachers may have been sometimes worn to cover the lacing on overbodies, as is possibly the case with the lady with the hen on the previous page [this may also be the case with the villager on page 146]. Here a flap appears to be either hooked or pinned across the front of her overbodies. This might have been sewn down or also hooked on the hidden other side. If the points are hooked another point of attachment would be required on each side near the waist to secure the flap in place.

While stomachers are almost unknown in common women's inventories, in London in 1611 it was ordered because of the "inordinate pride of mayde servauntes and women servauntes, in their excesse of apparel and follye in varietie of newe fashions" that "no maidservant or womanservant whatsoever dwelling or shall hereafter dwell within the city of London or the liberties thereof, which shall take any wages...[may]...wear any band, neckerchief, gorget, strippe or stomacher, but only plain,...nor any stomacher wrought with any gold, silver or silk, or with any other kind of stuff made with silk or mixed with silk."[69]. A lusty wench selling cheese and cream in the street in London in a 1601 ballad had "Her Bodyes and her Stomacher...fastened very tite."

Common women's stomachers appear to be plain, possibly matching the overbodies, and attached across the outside front of the overbody. Precise shapes are uncertain and possibly varied.

---

[69] Groc1611

Kirtles

A kirtle consisted of an overbody and a skirt, in some cases only the front half of a skirt. Like a petticoat it might have detachable sleeves and a stomacher. In the mortext 70% were of worsted and 15% of the rest of similar chamlets, grograins and mockadoes. 50% were red and 30% black with 10% blue and 10% tawney.

The panels of the kirtle skirt are symmetrical about the dotted line on the pattern and should be cut with the fabric folded along the warp or weft of the fabric. Three or four panels are required to make a complete kirtle depending on how full it was desired. Fore or half kirtles require two panels. Half kirtles would have a seam down the front which corresponds to the decoration seen on some garments. This is probably some form of tape or braiding obscuring the seam. A full kirtle may either have a seam down the front or a panel at the front.

Kirtle "Skirt"

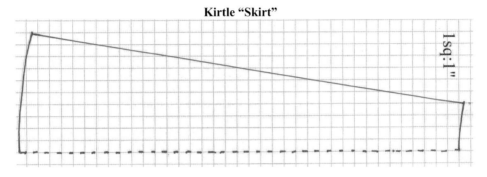

Kirtle Overbodies

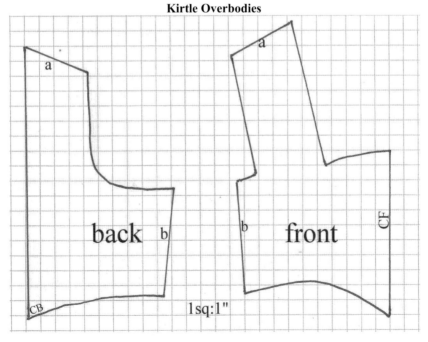

Kirtle 1570's

CP1579nlo[1.1a]

Kirtle in madder dyed say trimmed with black silk.
While definitely used in the 1570's this kirtle pattern may also apply more widely although dated images are unavailable.

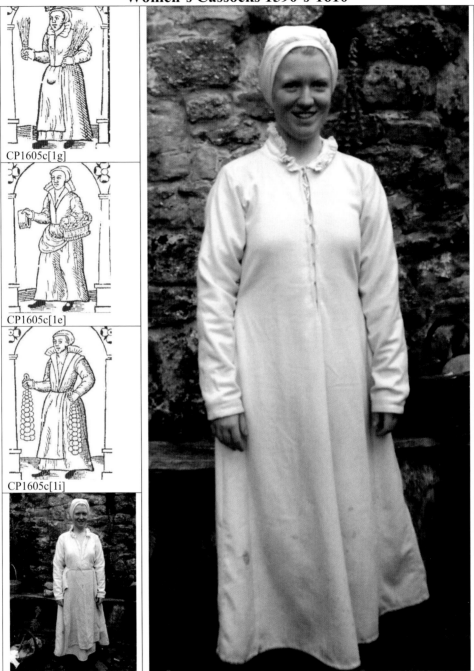

CP1605c[1g]

CP1605c[1e]

CP1605c[1i]

Woman's cassock in white woollen material with hooks and eyes down the front opening. The right picture is without an apron for clarity. In use an apron would always be worn to cover the lower part of the front slit. See page 47 for cassock with apron, open at the front.

Women's Cassocks

Women's cassocks were made from warm woollen material and two might be worn at once. 56% of those in the mortext were of russet and a further 33% frieze, the rest being kersie or broadcloth. Few if any seem to have been dyed although natural black may have been common. They could be closed with hooks and eyes up the front but were worn open to varying degrees. Normally an apron covered the lower part of the opening.

The picture and pattern show a version where the front and back are cut from one piece but they can alternatively be cut from two pieces with some shoulder shaping. Note this pattern requires 4 gores, 2 on each side.

Pattern for Woman's Cassock circa 1600

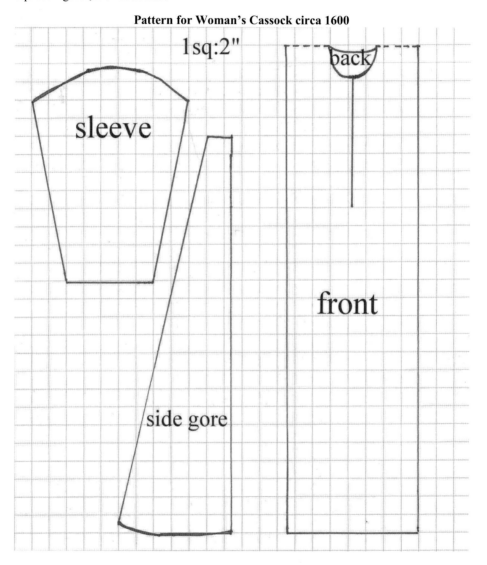

Chapter 8

Women's Waistcoats

Common women's waistcoats were almost entirely made of warm woollen materials. The predominant colours were white or red. Stammel is a variety of red.

Waistcoat Materials

Cotten	7	33%
Russet	4	19%
Stammel	3	14%
Flannel	2	10%
Selfgrow	1	5%
Kersey	1	5%
Woolen	1	5%
Linen	1	5%
Fustian	1	5%

Waistcoat Colours

Colour	Number	%	Notes
White	6	50%	
Red	3	25%	1 flannel, plus 1 set of red sleeves
Stammel	3	25%	

Waistcoat Patterns

Curved Sleeve, 5 Gored, Bays Waistcoat Pattern

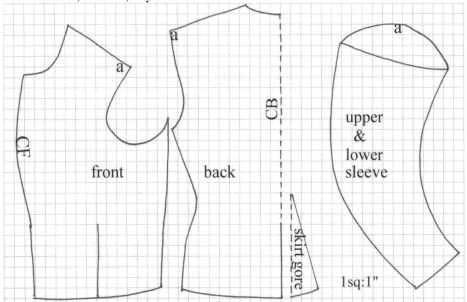

Check the length of the slits when the body pieces are assembled by trying on over the petticoat. They should extend up to the waist.

Women's Waistcoats

CP1635nl[1.1c]   CP1630nlo[1a]

Bays waistcoat with curved sleeves, gored skirt and hooks and eyes down the front opening.

Unlined cotton waistcoat with wide straight sleeves, a paneled skirt and hooks and eyes.

Waistcoat fronts are secured with hooks and eyes. Shoulder wings are optional with all designs. The various sleeve shapes can be used with each body pattern or optionally no sleeve at all.

More than one waistcoat can be worn at a time. The second might be worn under the overbody, tucked into the petticoat as is seen on some Dutch paintings.

Women's Waistcoats

CP1628nlo[1.1a]

Grey "Woollen" Cotton Waistcoat with a 5 Gored Skirt. Sleeveless with shoulder wing [right] or Narrow Straight Sleeved [left]. The skirt could be worn tucked into the petticoat if the petticoat is not sewn to the overbody [top left].

"Woollen" Cotton Sleeveless or Narrow Straight Sleeved
5 Gored Skirt Waistcoat Pattern

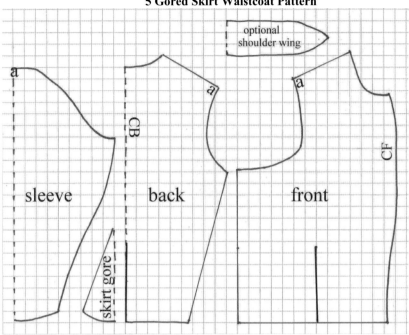

Wide Straight Sleeve, 9 Panel Skirt Waistcoat

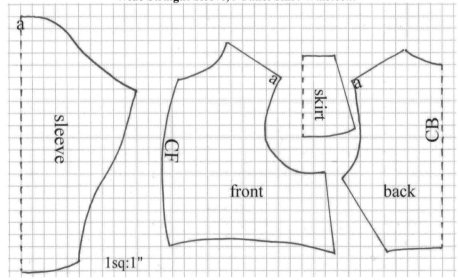

Women's Gowns[70]

Common Women's Gowns were full length sleeved garments normally made of warm woollen cloth. 68% were of russet and frieze.

Gown Materials

Russet	17	43%
Frieze	10	25%
Cloth	4	10%
Broadcloth	2	5%
Worsted	2	5%
Grogram	2	5%
Cotton	1	2%
Serge	1	2%
Lyell	1	2%
Buff	1	2%

Most gowns where a colour is mentioned are black, possibly due to mourning gowns being given to the poor. The white and sheep's russet gowns plus probably some of the black are undyed. As russet and frieze appears normally also to be undyed naturally pigmented cloth it is probable that a large majority of gowns are natural undyed shades of grey or brown.

Gown Colours

Black	16	62%
White	4	15%
Sheep's russet	2	8%
Violet	1	4%
Blue	1	4%
Green?	1	4%
Buff?	1	4%

Gowns for almshouses used between 3 and 6 yards of 26 inch wide frieze. Gowns were often lined in the body with canvas, buckram or for added warmth with woollen cotton. Russet gowns, probably for summer use, were sometimes mentioned as unlined.

Hooks and eyes were purchased for women's gowns almost certainly to fasten the front from neck to waist.

Decoration

In 1611 it was decreed that "no maidservant or woman servant whatsoever dwelling or shall hereafter dwell within the city of London or the liberties thereof, which shall take any wages or be hired or agree for ...[was not allowed to]... wear any gown, kirtle, waistcoat or petticoat of any kind of silk or stuff mingled with silk, nor any other stuff exceeding the price of 2s 6d [30d] a yard, nor any kersey exceeding the price of 5s [60d] a yard nor broad cloth exceeding the price of 10s [120d] a yard. **Nor any lace or guard upon her gown**, kirtle, waistcoat or petticoat, or any other garment, save only a cape [collar] of velvet". Some charity gowns were decorated with red guards or with the initials of the donor embroidered on the breast. A Sawyers wife had 18 yards of ribbon to dress her gown and a Yeoman's wife had a gown with fox fur but in general common women's gowns were probably undecorated.

---

[70] See Volume 22

Early Elizabethan Gown ungathered at the waist. 1570's

CP1570c[1]

Ungathered Russet Gown 1560's-1570's

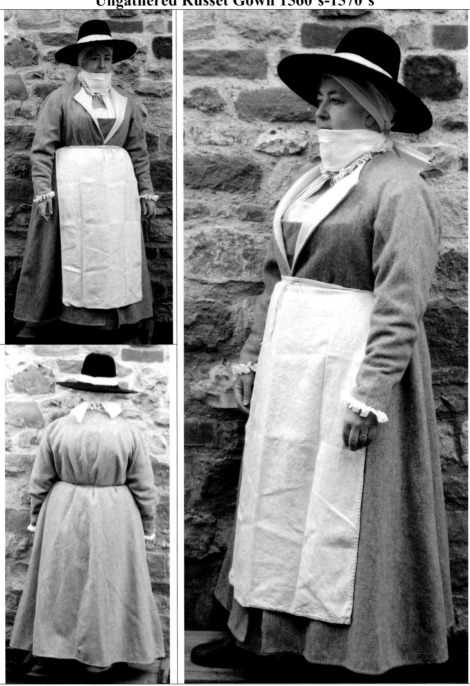

Ungathered grey russet gown lined along the front edge to the waist and at the cuffs only with white say. Worn over a madder red ungathered petticoat with stomacher.

Ungathered Russet Gown Pattern Circa 1570

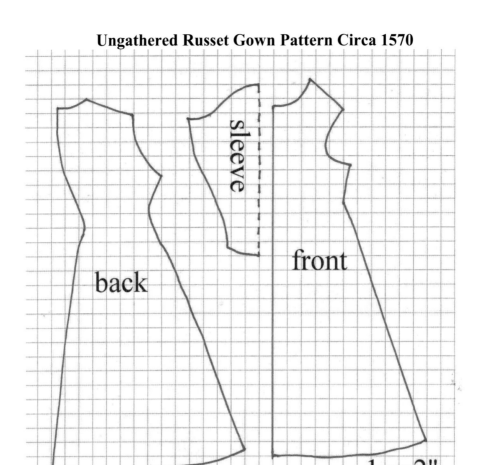

Gown Sleeves and Cuffs

Gowns might have sleeves, half sleeves which reached to the elbow, or be sleeved with another material such as buffen [a variety of grograin]. They could also have dedicated apparently detachable cuffs. The City of Bath in 1596 "paid [18d] for towe yeardes of red clothe to gard the almesfolkes gowne sleves". This was probably for 4 gowns giving 9 of material probably at least 36" wide for decorating each sleeve. This must have covered much of the surface area.

Gathered Russet or Frieze Gown with curved sleeves.
Circa 1590's onwards.

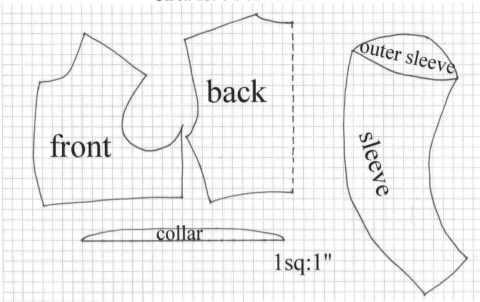

front

back

collar

outer sleeve

sleeve

1sq:1"

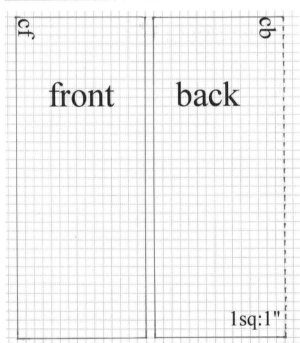

cf

front

back

cb

1sq:1"

Skirt of gown

Top of Gown

Collars and shoulder rolls are options.

Sleeves may be cut to half length and made tighter or looser as required.

A waistcoat pattern cut at the waist will serve as a gown top.

CP1598s[1.2d]

Later gowns gathered at the waist in russet [left] and frieze [right]. The upper body and sleeves of the frieze gown are lined with cotton for winter warmth. The front of the upper part of the russet gown is lined with say. Both fasten down the front to the waist with hooks and eyes.

Women's Cloaks 1610's to 1650's

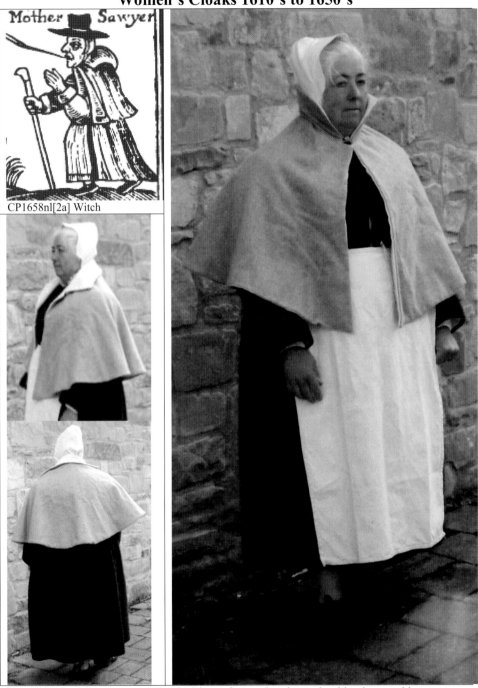

CP1658nl[2a] Witch

Woman's cloak in grey russet lined with say fastened at the neck with a loop and large button.

Women's Cloaks

The woman's cloak appears to be very similar to the man's except shorter and were probably like men's of russet lined with baize. A waist length semi circular cloak for a common woman of about 5'4" can be cut from 1 yard of 40.5 inch russet with 28" of 45" wide baize as lining.

Period of use: Although only referenced in 1600 and 1658 women's cloaks were possibly around throughout the period but uncommon. They were probably only used when away from the proximity of home travelling or working as shepherdesses.

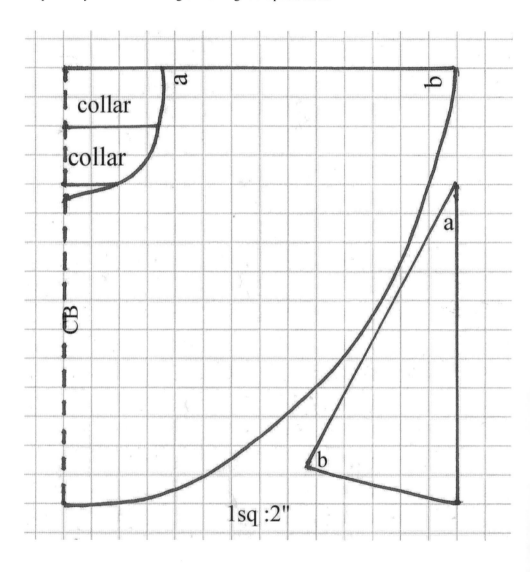

1sq :2"

Chapter 9
Women's Linens and Aprons

Common women wore a wide variety of linen garments on their heads, around their necks and next to their skin. Their aprons were also often of linen.

Headwear
Many of these garments were simple squares of linen the basic size, being probably a yard square [36" by 36"] although this could be subdivided into quarters or half either along the diagonals to make 2 or 4 smaller triangles or by dividing into 4 squares. Squares might be folded into triangles before being worn. These garments were known as kerchers, handkerchers, napkins, quarters and cross cloths. A circle or half circle, probably also based on a yard diameter, worn around the head or neck was called a rail.

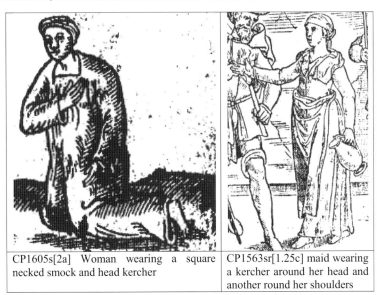

CP1605s[2a] Woman wearing a square necked smock and head kercher	CP1563sr[1.25c] maid wearing a kercher around her head and another round her shoulders

Some items were more complex. Neckerchers consisted of 3 parts, a body covering the upper chest, a neck band and a ruff or collar which could be in a finer fabric [see next page]. The whisk on page 55 is made from a rectangle of linen 10 inches by 68 inches gathered onto a neck band made from a strip of linen 3 inches by 17.5 inches.

Ruffs and Ruff Cuffs
Ruffs consist of a neck band onto which is tightly gathered a long strip of fine linen, hemmed on the outside edge. The same ruff band can be set in a number of ways but where visible the common women's ruffs are all set into a simple figure of eight pattern. Ruffs were set by first startching, drying and then ironing. It was then formed to shape with a hot poking iron and the evenly sized and spaced waves pinned into position. The reconstructed ruff on the following page was made of a strip 162 inches by 3.5 inches and a neck band 17" long by originally 4 inches wide but reduced to 1.5" wide after folding in half and sewing in the gathers. These gathers were as small and tight as possible, in the case of the reconstruction about 1/8th of an inch. Ruff cuffs were made in a similar fashion.

Womens Head and Neck Linens

Village Woman circa 1570 wearing 1] A Kercher under a hat. 2] A Face Kercher or Muffler. 3] A Neckercher with ruff, band and body. 4] A Rail over the shoulders.	Woman plucking a goose wearing a wired Coif and ruff Neckercher

Woman wearing a yard square kercher on her head and a rail around her shoulders

Rhino horn coif and kercher	Coif and rolled kercher	Wired coif

Ruffs and Cuffs

A ruff set and pinned

Woman with ruff and ruff cuffs

Ruff Cuffs

Large Circular Pleated Collar

Cuffs

Whisk

Women's Smocks

Women's smock's were mostly made of canvas or lockram. They used about 3.5 yards of material around 27"-36" wide.

Pattern for Square Necked Smock

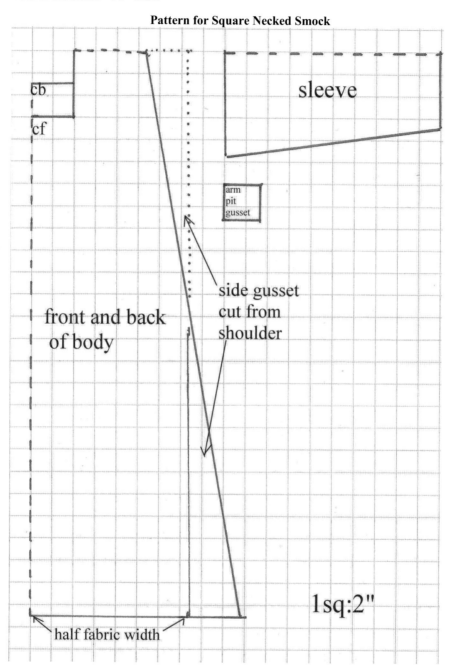

cb

cf

sleeve

arm
pit
gusset

front and back
of body

side gusset
cut from
shoulder

1 sq:2"

half fabric width

156

Pattern For *Front Slit* Smock

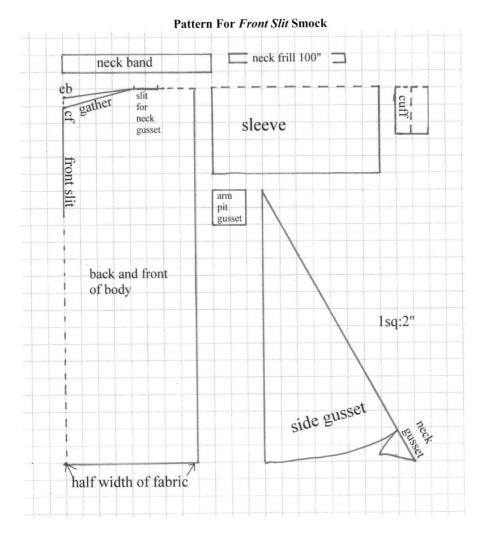

neck band

neck frill 100"

cb

slit for neck gusset

gather

cf

sleeve

cuff

front slit

arm pit gusset

back and front of body

1sq:2"

side gusset

neck gusset

half width of fabric

Constructing Smocks [both *Square Neck* and *Front Slit*]
The patterns show the cutting lines. The back and front of the body is cut in one piece, folding over the shoulder. Both smocks use a square gusset in each arm pit.

At the neck the body is gathered onto a neck band, optionally with a neck frill gathered onto it. Neck gussets are used in the slit front smock to improve the fit. The slit front smock has sleeves gathered onto cuffs.

The square neck smock has tapering sleeves loose at the wrists with no cuffs. These are an option on the Front Slit smock. With different width fabrics some measurements would have been adjusted to obtain the most economic use of fabric.

Women's Smocks

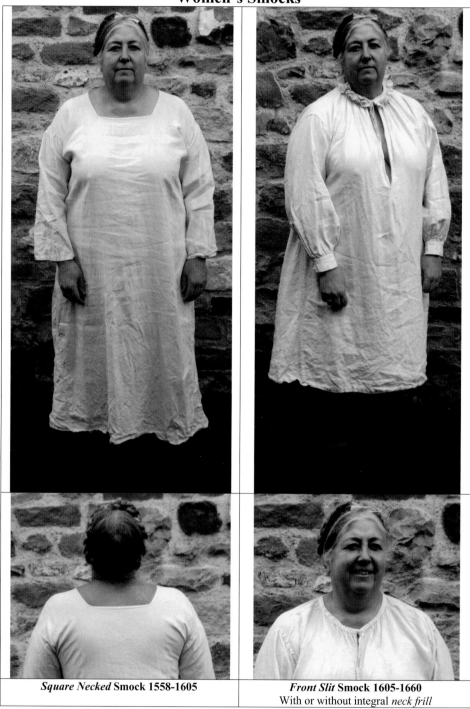

Square Necked Smock 1558-1605

Front Slit Smock 1605-1660
With or without integral *neck frill*

Women's Aprons

Women's working and market aprons. Note the "ear" beyond the ties, no indication of gathering and the apron strings tied at the front with a bow with a single loop

Linen apron with apron strings tied at the front with a single loop bow. 22 inches wide by 30 inches drop. The eyelets are 3 inches in from the top corners	Fine linen holiday apron gathered through a casement with a draw string tied at the front. 30 inches wide by 32 inch drop.	Sage green say apron, 23 inches wide by 31 inch drop, with madder dyed woolen braid. The apron is gathered with a draw string.

Women's Smocks

Women's smocks were mainly made of hemp either the courser canvas or better quality lockram. In one case a canvas smock had the more exposed sleeves in lockram. In general smocks seem to use between 3 and 3.75 yards of material probably between 27" and 36" wide.

There are two designs of smock, the *Square Neck* Smock and the *front slit*. The square neck is impractical for breast feeding but is not gathered and is smoother if wearing a neckercher over the smock. The wrists on these smocks do not show wrist bands and hang open.

CP1605c[1g]   CP1605c[1k]   CP1605c[1e]   CP1605c[1i]

The women above all wear a similar style cassock which, as it gradually opens, reveals that the smock underneath must have a very long front slit. The smock collar likewise stands up as the smock is turned back. This collar can vary in nature as the third woman shows it split between an inner and outer part. This might be interpreted as a narrow strip of linen gathered onto a band. The other three women show a wider collar or frill gathered onto the neck.

Women's Aprons

A common woman's apron was not a badge of domestic servitude but was probably essential for her modesty, covering the gap required to enable her to don her petticoat. In some cases it was an adornment to be worn on holidays. Nearly half the materials mentioned for women's aprons were thin woollen materials such as say and worsted which used combed, dense, worsted spun threads. These would have been difficult to wash regularly and were probably holiday aprons. There seems to have been a fashion for green say aprons although black is marginally more common and there are almost as many cheaper blue aprons possibly woad dyed linen. The worsted aprons all pre date and the say all post date 1600. The majority of aprons were probably plain white linen and most are shown undecorated although a few have braids or tape borders. Aprons were attached by strings tied off with a single loop bow at the front [see previous page]. The point of attachment of the strings is often part way along the top edge [see the Goose plucker's apron on the previous page]. Many aprons appear gathered in illustrations.

Children's Clothing[71]

With the exception of women when they marry the clothing of common people undergoes no significant changes after they leave home at around the age of 14. Children in the family home, in contrast, undergo a series of developmental changes and their clothing alters significantly, especially during the early years.

The newborn common child is clearly swaddled in the period illustrations. This starts as complete envelopment:	 CP1635nl[1.2c]	 CP1607s[1d]
....but soon the arms are freed while the torso and legs are still bound. The head appears covered with a biggin a form of coif. High status images of biggin normally show them tied under the chin with linen tapes.	 CP1602c[1c]	 CP1602c[1c]
This child appears to have a biggin with a frill or lace, and a frill around it's neck, probably on a shirt.	 CP1632nlo[1c]	 CP1632nlo[1c]
A slightly older child being lowered by its mother from a burning house in the great fire of Tiverton in 1612 appears to wear a loose, shirt like, garment reaching to ankles and wrist and with a slit down the front. There is presumably a slit at the side which has allowed the leg to protrude. The horizontal lines across the chest are to represent the rope.	 CP1612s[1d]	 CP1607s[1c]

---

[71] For full details on children's clothing see Volume 24.

Babies Clothing

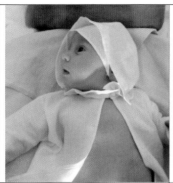 

| Baby with fine linen cross cloth and biggin [coif] on its head. Evidence for is from the 1660's cross cloths and of uncertain status. | Baby in a front opening shirt with a frill at the neck and a breach clout made from a square of linen [aprox 24 inches per side] tied around with linen tape. The front opening shirt is conjectural but far eaisier to put on a new born. |

Swaddling a Baby: new born

   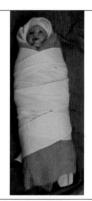

| Baby in linen shirt and breech clout | Linen biggin and sheet added | Wrapped in woolen blanket | Linen swaddling strip aprox. 144" by 3" |

Swaddling a Baby: age 9 weeks

 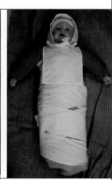

With the arms free this child required a waistcoat, in this case of madder dyed baize lined with buckthorn dyed fustian. Like the shirt this waistcoat is open all along its length for ease of dressing		
	Plus biggin and forehead cloth	Plus linen bib

Boy's Long Coat

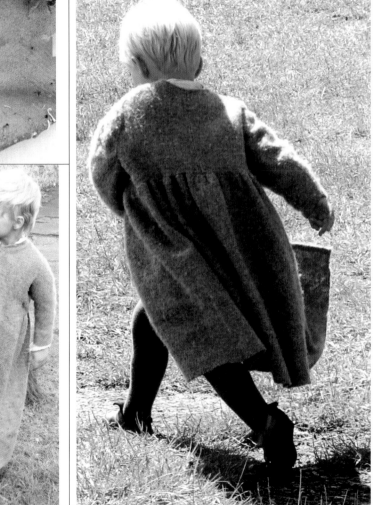

A garment discovered in Abingdon [right], estimated to fit a 4-6 year old boy, may represent the upper part or upper body of a boy's long coat. It might alternatively be part of a doublet for an older breeched child of small stature.

The Abingdon garment had at least 18 buttonholes down the front with thread buttons. The outer layer was a blue kersey with a fustian liner and an interliner. The collar was stiffened with pasteboard[72].

Boy's long coat in gray cotton worn over a linen shirt. The boy is 4 on the right and 6 on the left. The coat has been expanded with additional inserts as the child grew.

---

[72] See Volume 24 for full details and pattern

Long Coats for Boys

Once they were able to walk clothing appears to differentiate for boys and girls, although young common boys still wore a gown like garment until probably around the age of 7-8. This was probably called a long coat. During the 1607 floods on the South Wales coast "a man Child of the age, of 5. or 6. yeares, which was kept swimming for the space of two hours, above the waters, by reason that his long Coates lay spread upon the tops of the waters"[73]. Christ's Hospital in Ipswich in 1596 provided "2 long coats the overbodys beinge lynide with canvas" each for some of the boys in its care. They also purchased tin buttons and "Lether lacis to sett on the buttones of the boyes cotes". Other boys, probably older, received jerkins and breeches while the girls received frocks or petticoats. The implication is that these long coats were of 2 parts joined together, an over body with a canvas lining and a lower portion. These coats were closed down the front, at least on the upper part, with tin buttons. The following illustration may show boys in such garments under which they seem to wear a long shirt. Some of the overbodies appear to have tabs.

| CP1625nlo[3f] | CP1634nlo[2] | CP1638nlo[1] | CP1622nl[1a] |

After the age of about 7 boys were breeched and wear miniature versions of adult male clothing. The Reigate doublet on page 54 fits a boy of 9.

Frocks for Young Girls

At Christ Hospital in 1596 the "grete wenches" were provided with petticoats, overbodies and wastecoats, similar garb to adult women. Other Girls presumably the younger ones received frocks "the overbody beinge lynide". The child in black in the 1638 illustration above wears a head kercher and may be a girl in such a frock.

Adult common women in the earlier Elizabethan period were also recorded with frocks but the exact nature of these garments is uncertain. The adult frocks were made of russet and frieze and may have been similar to women's cassocks.

---

[73] CP1607s[1]   STC 1850 57

Chapter 10
Accessories

Stockings

Period stocking could be either knitted or made out of woven cloth.

Knitted Stockings
Knitted stockings could be made out of a variety of thread. Carded woollen stockings from chunky yarn were generally cheapest while those knitted from combed worsted wool yarn or Jersey yarn were more expensive and silk stockings extremely expensive. Knitted stockings for soldiers in 1642 weighed about 9oz per pair. Some female farm servants were given wool so that they could knit their own stockings.

Cloth Stockings
These could be made from a variety of materials. Kersey was common probably because the twill weave provided enough stretch to pull on reasonably close fitting stockings. Frieze stockings, possibly also known as Irish stockings, would have been very warm and were recommended for troops for winter wear in Ireland. While the New Model Army mainly ordered Irish stockings in 1645, in 1646 they experimented with woollen stockings cut from "good welsh cotton".

Stocking Colours
Common men owned stockings in a range of colours:

Colour	Stockings	Of which	Netherstocks comparison
Blue	6	2 knit	3
Green	3		
Straw	1	1 knit	
Orange	1		
White	3	3 knit	1
Black	1	1 knit	1 black russet

Stockings were sent out to be dyed already made and some stockings appear to be dyed as a cottage industry by widows rather than the big commercial dyers.

Wearing stockings

The tops of stockings could be worn either under or over the knees of the breeches. They were often supported by garters either above or below the knee. Common men's garters were normally a single strip round the leg tied with a bow with a single loop while the elite often used a turn above and another below the knee, a style which may have extended to the very richest common men.

Stockings

Top left: Knitted undyed coarse woolen stockings [Gunnister pattern] with madder dyed garters below the knee.

Top Right: Old, buckthorn dyed, knitted stockings.

Bottom left: Natural black Irish Frieze *trumpet* stockings worn right with garters over the knee.

Below: Women's Short stockings made from madder dyed red woollen cotton cloth.

Garters

Garters are shown worn by common men either just below the knee or optionally just above if the stockings are worn over the knees of the breeches. Double garters which do both appear to be the normally preserve of the elite although a pair can be seen on London Trained Band musketeer in the 1580's [right].

Garters are normally shown tied with a single bow [bottom left]. They could be made of a woven strip of worsted, woollen, linen or silk tape

CP1587s[1.2z]

CP1605c[1f]

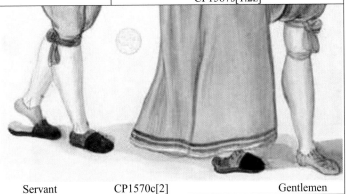

Servant   CP1570c[2]   Gentlemen

Gloves

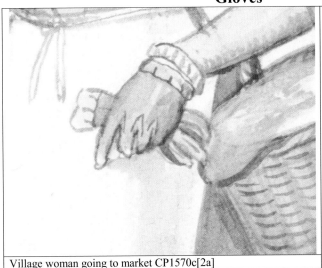

Village woman going to market CP1570c[2a]

Gloves had a variety of uses, both practical, such as hedging and harvesting, and ceremonial such as gifts at marriages and funerals. This led to the use of differing materials as well as a range of qualities and designs.

Gloves were often made of leather, typically sheep, calf, deer, goat and dog skins. They could also be knitted or made from woven cloth and could be furred.

Glover's inventories sometimes differentiated women's gloves from men's.

Making Cloth Cut Stockings

Guide Patterns for:
Left: Above knee frieze *trumpet* hose for size 7 feet   Right: Shorter hose for size 5 feet

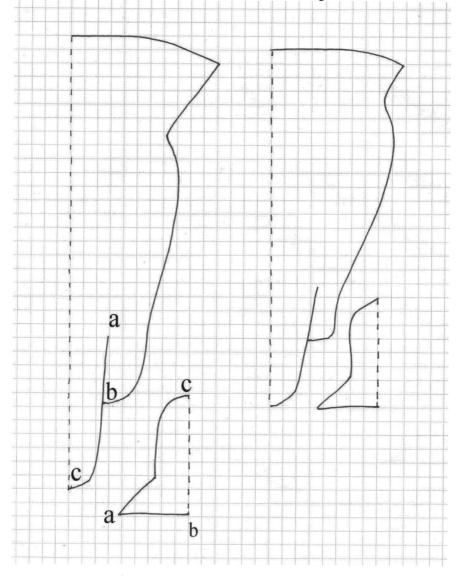

Scale 1sq:1"

Hose need to fit your legs closely and a pattern can be made to your own measurements. Remember to pre-shrink fabric. Frieze is so heavily finished that it does not need to be cut on the cross. Frieze hose are not as tightly fitted.

Headwear[74]

Headwear, other than linen, was split into two types, caps and hats.

Caps

Under the 1570 Statute of Caps, repealed in 1598, all common people over the age of 6, except maidens, must "wear on the sabath and Holiday unless in the time of their Travel...upon their head one cap of wool knit, thicked and dressed in England." There were many types of knitted woollen caps which would fulfill this requirement. Knitted caps underwent a number of processes including fulling which felted the surface and in many cases it was probably not at first obvious that the cap was knitted.

The Labourer's Cap and The Night Cap
The labourer's cap, so named by Randal Holmes in 1688, is shown on working men. It differs from the night cap only in having a button on the top.

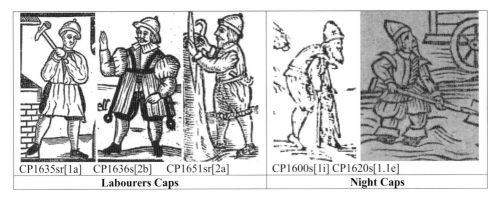

CP1635sr[1a] CP1636s[2b] CP1651sr[2a]	CP1600s[1i] CP1620s[1.1e]
Labourers Caps	**Night Caps**

Many variations are shown of such caps some of which may be linen rather than knitted wool.

"Flat Caps"
Various styles of flat cap had been in use from earlier in the Tudor period. At this period they are shown with or without a brim.

CP1568s[1] CP1640s[1.20]	CP1624s[2a] CP1640s[1.10]
With Brim	**Without Brim**

---

[74] See Volume 19

Monmouth Caps

Monmouth caps weighed about 1lb and cost around 24d probably about 4 times the weight and price of labourer's caps. They were lined and very rare in wills and inventories but common in purchases for soldiers going to Ireland and American colonists. The one probable illustration of a Monmouth cap is on a butcher in 1642 although Holmes calls this a knit cap.

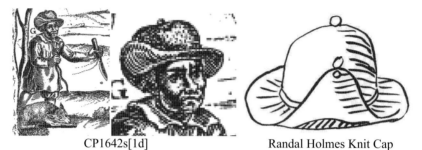

CP1642s[1d]   Randal Holmes Knit Cap

The brim of the cap is buttoned to the side to produce the turn up

Northern Blue Bonnets

A Northumberland tenant farmer was illustrated "with a good blue bonnet":

CP1633s[1.2a]   CP1633s[1.3a]

Women's Caps

It is difficult to separate caps in illustrations of women from linen headwear with certainty. The most probable sighting is a witch in 1579. Some women's caps were white.

CP1579s[1.1a] suspected witches   CP1579s[1b] witches

Montero Caps

These are the odd man out of period caps appearing to be made from woven cloth and not knitted. They could be pulled down to hide the face or turned up, possibly like a balaclava, and appear to have two brims. They were probably not used in England before 1620 and may have been largely restricted to Royalist troops with the Oxford army in 1643.

| RHAA | Royalist Officer | CP1652s[2.1a] |

Hats

Hats were made from a variety of materials, including straw, woven fabrics over a cardboard former and felt, and came in a wide variety of shapes. Some probably had wire shaping the brims. Shop inventories could be divided into "felts" and "hats".

Straw Hats

John Aubrey in "The Natural History of Wiltshire" remarked that "Before the civill Warres [pre 1642] I remember many of them [shepherds] made straw hatts". There is evidence that they tied beneath the chin, could be lined and were made of rye straw. As well as summer work they are associated by Shakespeare in the Tempest with holiday use and were worn with city badges on midsummer processions in London.

Possible straw hats.

CP1630nlo[1a]		
Haymaker	**Shepherd**	**London Street Seller**

The only ready made garment imported into England in significant numbers was the straw hat. In 1567-8 46,800 coarse straw hats and 2,400 fine straw hats arrived in London from Antwerp. Nearly all arrived between late March and the beginning of May, ready to be sold as the warmer weather approached.

Fabric Hats

Stubbes in his Anatomy of Abuses in 1583 wrote of women's hats: "Every artefacers wife (almost) wil not stick to goe in her hat of Velvet everyeday, every marchants wife, and meane gentlewoman, in her French-hood, and everye poore Cottagers Daughter, in her taffetie hat or els of woll at least, wel lined with silk, velvet or taffatie…"

While the merchant's wife and mean gentlewoman with their French hoods are above the definition of common women the implication or claim is that craftsmen's wives wore hats covered in velvet and cottagers daughters [part of the rural poor] wore hats of taffeta or probably felted wool lined with silk, velvet or taffeta.

Some Fabric Hat Styles

CP1579nlo[1.1b]   CP1591s[1a]   CP1570c[1]

Felt Hats

Common people's felt hats were made of sheep's wool sometimes blended with imported wool with better felting properties. This Ostrich wool was from Austria [Osterich] not as some modern sources state from the underdown of ostriches. Both white and gray wool was imported and hats were often dyed.

Hat Styles

In many cases it is uncertain from illustrations whether a hat is felt or fabric. Hats could have round or flat topped crowns of varying heights, bulbous tops, tapering sides, varying widths of brims and so forth.

Some Women's Hat Styles

| CP1563sr[1.15b] | CP1581nl[1.1a] | CP1598s[1.13c] | CP1620nl[1e] | CP1652nlo[1a] |

*Macarell new: Maca_rell*	Many women have broad brimmed, flat topped hats. This may be due to the English woman's habit of carrying heavy loads such as baskets of fish or fruit or pails of milk on the head.
CP1640s[1.17]	 *Any Milke heere*
	CP1635s[1a] CP1655s[1h]

There was a wide variety of hats shapes and even when a group of people seem to be wearing hats of similar shape they have normally personalised them often by bending the brims up or down in a wide variety of different ways.

London Trained Bandsmen at the State Funeral of Sir Phillip Sydney 1587

Some Male Hat Styles

				Presbyterian
CP1570c[2]	CP1587s[1.1j]	CP1620sr[1a]	CP1636s[2a]	CP1647s[1a]
CP1577nl[1]	CP1592s[1.1]	CP1624s[1b]	CP1640s[1.3]	CP1653s[1a]

Hat Bands

Not all hats had external bands although probably the majority did. Hat bands came in a wide variety of styles from strips of cloth possibly silk [See Sir Phillip Sydney's funeral above] to twisted cords in two colours or copper. One Devon yeoman in 1596 bought 30 gold "buttons" to decorate his hatband. Bands of leather or taffeta could also be found inside the brim of hats.

Feathers

	Feathers are rare in hats in illustrations of common people. Most look like small sprays of native birds, possibly cockerel's feathers in the longer cases. A very few look like ostrich feathers which might cost half a day's wages each for a labourer.	
Street vendor 1640		**Outlaws CP1605nl[1]**

Hair on the head

Men

Illustrations from the period make it clear that, while most wore hats or caps most of the time, it was not uncommon for common Englishmen to be bare headed both at work, leisure and more formal occasions. No evidence was found that they wore wigs at this period. Most common men's hair is collar length or shorter, only the military seeming to have a propensity for long flowing locks. Beards seem normal but not universal for those over 22, many younger men possibly struggling to grow a respectable beard.

Women

Women are almost always shown with some form of head covering. This is often linen rather than a woollen cap or hat[75]. Where hair is shown it is worn long, sometimes dressed into braids wound around the back of the head. This is probably the normal arraignment of the hair under head linens.

---

[75] Linens, including head coverings, are dealt with in Chapter 9.

Footwear[76]

Footwear at the period consisted mainly of shoes, calf length farmer's boots and knee length boots. The style of shoes changed gradually over the period. In the early part of Elizabeth's reign the footwear consisted entirely of slip on shoes, by the 1580's latchet shoes start to be seen but slip on shoes can still be seen in illustrations up to the mid 1630's.

Variant styles of Slip On Shoes

CP1570c[1] Villager

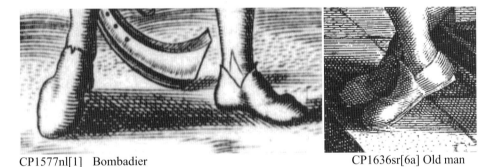

CP1577nl[1]   Bombadier   CP1636sr[6a] Old man

New styles do not come in and immediately replace the old but there are long periods where both styles of shoe can be seen on common people.

A child's "17th century" shoe found in the Royal Grammar School Guildford, built in 1575.

While the stylistic dating must be considered suspect this shoe does conform to many of the images in the corpus showing latchet style and a wedged heel without a stepped heel. This may well have been a common child's shoe from the period 1580-1660 but also could possibly come from outside those limits.

---

[76] See Volume 20.

The use of stepped heels on shoes took even longer to become widespread. The first record is in 1595 when the queen is recorded with "spanyshe lether shoes with highe heels with arches". By 1611 London Apprentices were being forbidden to wear shoes with heels but the first illustrations of shoes with arched heels worn by common people cannot be identified until the early 1640's and flat soled shoes are still shown at the end of the period in the 1650's.

Latchet Shoes without Heels in the 1650's

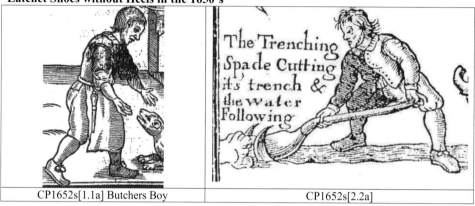

CP1652s[1.1a] Butchers Boy	CP1652s[2.2a]

Latchet Shoes with Stepped Heels

CP1651s[1b] Maidservant	CP1651s[1d] Soldier	CP1653s[1a]

Lefts and Rights
Archaeological evidence from Virginia 1607-8 and Pontefract Castle 1645-49 shows that while some pairs of shoes were made straight, i.e. no left or right, more were made with left and right hand shaped shoes.

Hob nails

Hob nails were used on some shoes by both men and women. Leather soles on dry grass become very polished and slippery while hob nails on stone flag or tile floors not only damage the floor but slide dangerously. Hob nailed shoes were probably generally for outdoor use and plain soles for indoors.

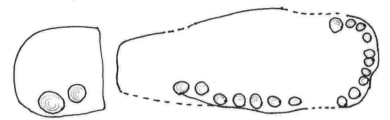

Hobnail pattern on a shoe sole from Pontefract Castle deposited 1645-9

Pantofles.

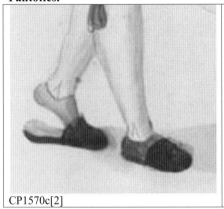

CP1570c[2]

Pantofles were a backless overshoe used to keep normal footwear clean while negotiating mucky streets. They could be easily kicked off when the destination was reached but had to be frequently kicked against hard objects to prevent them slipping off while walking. They might also be kept under the bed at night in case of need.

1640

Calf Length Boots

Throughout the whole period the stereotype of the farmer or farm worker is a man with calf length boots. These are always shown without a heel, even in 1660.

1642 A shepherd in calf length boots. The objects seen in the sole plates on the right boot may be hobnails or wooden pegs securing the plates.

Knee Length Boots

Up until the 1620's knee length boots are shown as a straight black tube often with a white turn down top which is probably the boot hose rather than the boot. They are mostly shown worn with spurs attached or by postmen on horseback and may normally be used for riding although similar boots on farmers draining a pond may be known as "water boots".	 CP1620sr[1a]
 CP1655s[1v]	By the late 1620's a style today called the *bucket top boot* is described. While probably mainly a riding boot and shown on cavalry this was also a fashion item used by some townies for walking in and first appears in pictures of common English soldiers and Hackney Coachmen around 1649 and onwards.

Buckled Shoes

Between 1550 and 1608 there are a number of references to yellow or copper shoe buckles on common men or to buckles for shoemakers costing around of a third of a penny each. Some may actually be on calf length boots. None have been seen in illustrations and they may be a relatively uncommon Elizabethan feature.

Chapter 11

Replicating Elizabethan and Early Stuart Clothing[77]

Construction Instruction: Using the Patterns

The patterns given in this book show the stitching lines and have no seam allowance so that the sewing line can be drawn onto the fabric. The seam allowance required may vary with the type of material used. To adjust the outlines of the patterns in this book to the size of your body use the instruction in Volume 1 Appendix 1. You may do this on a photocopy of the pattern producing a new outline. Next transfer this adjusted pattern onto transparent paper laid over a large sheet of 1" squared paper or a cutting board marked out with 1 inch squares. Where there is a fold line on the pattern you will need to use transparent paper folded in half as this panel is symmetrical along the fold line and is twice the size of the shape in the pattern. Ensure that you place the fold line of the pattern along the folded edge of the paper not the open edge.

Cut out the pattern pieces. Only the pieces for one side [left or right] of the garment are shown. All pieces will need a mirror image for the other side [unless they have a fold line in which case the mirror half is already attached on the other side of the folded piece of paper]. Carefully mark the outside faces of the pattern pieces. The pattern pieces in this book are not laid out as a cutting diagram as the widths of materials will vary significantly. Arrange the pattern pieces on your material efficiently and mark round. When you cut allow a seam allowance outside this line.

Panels may be made up by sewing on a small piece [piecing] if this saves waste. This was a common practice even on elite garments. Where possible cut the main panels so that the grain of the fabric runs in the same direction either up and down the garment or across.

Many patterns are shown with the front and back superimposed. They can be cut with a side seam or, where straight, a fold at this point. Depending upon the width of the fabric more seams could be needed preferably in the back half of the panel.

Breeches linings can be much narrower than the outer layer. The lining is usually inserted after breeches have been constructed. The waistband can be lined separately or a longer lining used, attaching to the top of the waistband, this is easier when the lining does not have to be gathered very much.

Key to Pattern Diagrams	
Dotted lines represent a fold. Where the two sides of the fold differ these are shown superimposed.	
Lines of alternate dots and dashes represent the edges of lining pieces where they differ from the outer.	
CF	Centre Front
CB	Centre Back

---

[77] A more detailed analysis of the methods used at the period and how to replicate them can be found in Volume 1 part 2

Use of fabric

Linen garments are almost entirely composed of pieces bounded by straight lines, mainly following the direction of the warp and weft. Surviving elite shirt and smocks such as the Slingsby shirt[78], the shirt from the Abingdon Collection[79] and a smock in the V&A[80] use the width of the fabric, selvedge to selvedge, for the main body. Quantities of fabric recorded for common folk's smocks and shirts indicate that this was likely to be normal.

Drawing out a thread from the warp or weft is a probable way in which straight lines were defined along the warp or weft to follow when cutting. Folding and creasing could be used to easily mark a diagonal.

Many garments consist of multiple layers which can be defined as follows:

Outer Layer – The visible outside fabric.
2nd outer layer – Rarely present in common peoples' clothing. This is seen if outer layer is slashed or pinked revealing a decorative under layer.
Interliner- coarse, open weave hemp, linen or wool used to back the *outer layer* or layers. Open, plain weave, *interliners* stretch and conform to the cut of the *outer layer*. *Interliners* may be used in multiple layers in areas such as the collar, shoulders and fronts[81]. Evidence for interlining is restricted to doublets and breeches.
Stiffening- A rigid, stiff layer of material such as pasteboard[82] used in collars and other parts where stiffness and rigidity are required.

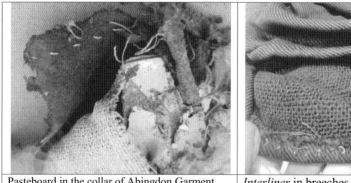 

| Pasteboard in the collar of Abingdon Garment | *Interliner* in breeches 1625-35 V&A[83] |

Padding- Bombast may have been used to pad out some common men's doublets[84]. Bombast was probably cotton wool for the elite but may have been coarser fibers for common people[85]. It is thought to be unwoven material.
Lining- The internal face. It neatens, protects, strengthens and makes the garment warmer.

---

[78] Knaresborough Castle
[79] Museum of London 1581-1590 **ID no:** 28.84
[80] V&A English embroidered smock ca. 1630 **Museum number** T.2-1956
[81] E.g. in the Reigate doublet see vol. 10&11
[82] Layers of linen paper pasted together. See Vol. 2 Haberdashery.
[83] Museum number: T.29&A-1938
[84] See vol. 10&11 Doublets
[85] See vol. 2 Haberdashery

Sewing

Four Basic Stitches are mentioned at the period: Fore stitch, Back stitch, Whip stitch and Privy stitch. Additional Sewing Adjectives can be used to describe variations that can be used on the above stitches. Stitches can be described as long or short or as "Stabbing" where the thread enters and leaves the fabric at 90 degrees to the surface or "Catching" where the thread goes partially through the fabric, to show as little as possible on the other side.

Fore stitch

A stitch where the thread proceeds continually in a forward direction. It is usually an even stitch both on the right side and reverse of the fabric. It was used for gathering and holding layers together and could have been used for seams and basting. It is fast, easy and economic in thread use. If used alone for seams, it can pull apart in places where there is tension, causing the rest of the seam to gather.

In some fabrics multiple passes can be made through the fabric with the needle before the thread is pulled through, this makes it a very fast stitch, especially useful when gathering. When doing this the needle and therefore the stitches enter and leave the fabric at a shallow angle.	

As seen above, when fabric was to be gathered, fore stitch could be used, the length of the stitch is dependent upon the size of the required gathers. A paper guide is useful to ensure even and correct size stitches. Although only one row of stitches can be seen on these garments more than one row of parallel stitches is usually needed to control the gathers properly.

Stabbing Fore Stitch

A variation can be made with a stabbing action where the stitch goes straight through at 90 degrees to the fabrics rather than being angled. Useful for thick or stiff fabrics.

In gathering, the fabric can be folded on to the needle where it is easier to make a straight pass through the fabric.	Stabbing fore stitch is also useful for holding layers together without slippage.

Diagonal Fore Stitch

This can be done either at an angle, diagonal fore stitch, or vertically as stabbing diagonal fore stitch. The latter would be visible on both sides and is therefore more likely to be used to hold interlining layers together or for temporary basting. If fore stitch is worked in a series of diagonal passes, layers, such as interlining or padding, can be held together without slippage or gathering.

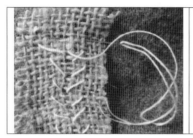

Diagonal fore stitch worked from the reverse side, only picking up a few threads from the back of the outer fabric, the stitching should not be visible on the right side.

Back Stitch

Back stitch worked continuously with stitches touching.

By itself, or in combination with fore stitch, back stitch is the most useful stitch for seams. It is a strong form of stitching allowing some elasticity in the seam, so the thread is less likely to break under pressure. It is more difficult to remove so less useful for temporary stitching.

A combination of fore stitch and back stitch is fairly fast and economic, using less thread than full backstitch and avoids the problem of unwanted gathering that you can get with fore stitch alone.

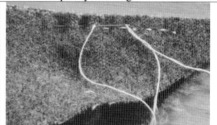

Open Back Stitch

An open back stitch worked from the right side using tiny, barely visible stitches is useful for top stitching.

Stabbing Open Back Stitch

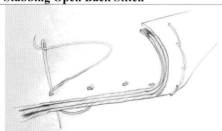

Worked from the right side, the needle is worked in single passes at 90 degrees to the wad of fabric

Couching Back Stitch or Couching Fore Stitch

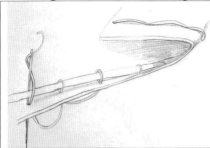

A thread or cord, laid on the surface, can be couched, or attached to the surface using open backstitch stitch, fore stitch or, as a third option, the needle can return through the fabric where the sewing thread comes out.

This can be a decorative feature but is also used to reinforce seam stitching. Thicker stronger thread can be used than can fit through the needle's eye. It will also prevent the seam from stretching out of shape.

Whip Stitch

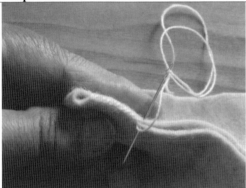

Whip stitch is worked over the edge of the fabric and can make a strong seam. The stitches are worked closely together so that they touch. It is used for joining selvedges and hemmed or folded edges and making eyelets. It uses minimal seam allowance.

When used, not too tightly, the seam can be opened flat after working and therefore the edges are 'butt' joined.

Eyelets

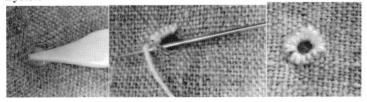

A hole is made by forcing threads apart with an awl and the edge whip stitched.

Open Whip Stitch

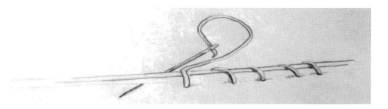

Open is a variation of whip stitch where the stitches are further apart. It has the advantage of speed and when used to seam is not so rigid.

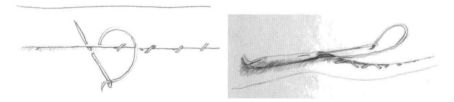

A form of open whip stitch was used to hem material. In this case the slanting stitch was worked on the reverse side, as in the diagram above, just catching the fabric so that it barely shows on the right side. This may be what is called at the period Privy Stitch or Fine Drawing

Blanket Whip Stitch

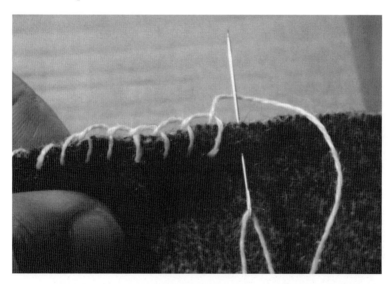

This can be worked on folded or raw edges. It is used to neaten edges to avoid fraying.

Buttonhole Whip Stitch

This is similar to the stitch above, but worked closely with the stitches touching. It can stretch slightly.

Button loops were sometimes made in this fashion as an alternative to buttonholes in places like collars that were too stiff [with pasteboard] to work buttonholes.

Multiple worked thread loops as a continuous edge are used as an alternative to a casing for gathering on coifs, they cause less damage to the fabric and are easy to replace when they wear.

Buttonhole whip stitch is an alternative to whip stitch around an eyelet.

Garment Construction

Hemming

Some common men's woollen garments may not normally have been hemmed. Garments made from less finished fabric may have been in more need of hemming and linens certainly would have been hemmed.

Seams

Simple seams using one line of stitching have been covered above. Many heavily finished woollen fabrics such as frieze, broadcloth and kersies do not tend to fray when cut and can be seamed with one line of stitching[86]. More open woollen fabrics, such as cottons, and linens are prone to fraying at the edges unless there is a selvedge. They may require seams with more than one row of stitching.

Top Stitching

Top stitching is useful for holding seams back, it makes them flat and when under pressure, less likely to pull the fabric threads apart and fray.

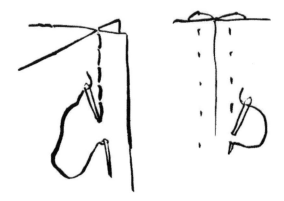

Run and Fell Seams

This is often used on linens. Two rows of stitching are used. First either back stitch or fore stitch is used to hold the two panels together [left hand row of stitching]. Next one side of the seam allowance is then folded under and hemmed [right hand row of stitching].

---

[86] The Dungivin Costume by A Henshall and W Seaby. Ulster Museum.

Forms of Gathering

Gathering onto a Band
Even fore stitches can be used to gather and reduce a long length of fabric to the length of the band or panel it is to be joined to. It is then stitched in place with fore or back stitch.

Cartridge Pleating

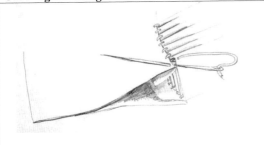

In Cartridge pleating both edges of the gathers are sewn separately to a band or panel. This results in firm, structural pleating where a lot of fabric length is reduced to a little.	The folds can be sewn to a tape to hold their form. For more bulk this can be worked with hemmed or folded-in fabric

Flat Pleating

This is achieved by overlapping at regular intervals to reduce the excess fullness. This gives a flatter 'gather' which sticks out as little as possible. The folds can all go the same way or change direction part way round the garment to give a symmetrical effect.	

Easing

Easing is gathering without any pleats or visible folds. It can be used around armholes, necks, edging and other curved seams where it is desirable to have slightly more length in one piece of fabric than the piece it is to be joined to. It is commonly used when setting in sleeves.	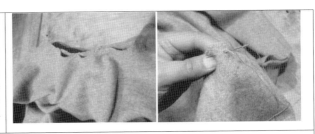

This is achieved by sewing whilst the long side (sleeve head) is bent around the shorter side (armhole) as the seam progresses.

Darts

Darts are used on linens such as collars and cuffs to shape the rectangle to fit a band.	

Casing

A casing is a tube created in the hemmed edge of the panel for a drawstring to be inserted through allowing for variable gathering. There is no evidence of this form of gathering being used on smock necks, petticoat waists or cuffs. This may be because it tends to wear the fabric badly.	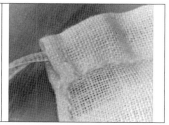

Binding

To bind an edge tape is sewn on to the right side of the fabric using back stitch. The tape is then folded over to the inside, turned in and hemmed. For curved seams binding cut on the cross of the weave is preferable as it can stretch.

Attaching Tape Ties

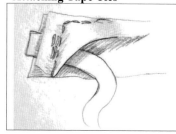	The tape is inserted in the seam [left], and firmly sewn down, so that on turning it emerges from the seam [right].	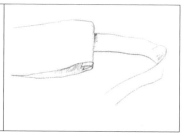

Attaching Strings

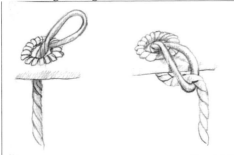

Strings for bands, cuffs and aprons can be attached by looping through eyelet holes.

Attaching Hooks and Eyes

The stitch used for attaching hooks and eyes is covered under whip stitch in "Stitches". The lining, attached afterwards, can hide the attachment portion of the hooks and eyes

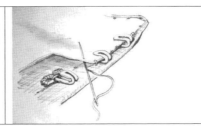

.

Sewing on Thread Buttons

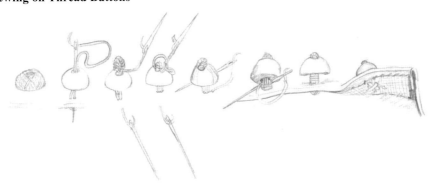

These are sewn on, with strong threads that go through the core, leaving a space between the fabric and button. At the top of the button the thread loop is whipped with thick thread. Two passes through the fabric and button give a cross at the top]. The exposed holding threads under the button are then whipped with linen thread, making a fairly rigid shank. The thread is fastened underneath.

Appendix 1
Short Glossary[87]

Term	Description
Baise	A half worsted, half woollen cloth
Binding	Some type of tape sown around the edge of a garment such as at the neck or pocket holes.
Braid	Woven tape
Broadcloth	Usually between 58" and 63" wide, quality cloth, well finished
Corpus Pictorum	The body of validated images of English common people from the period. See next page for details.
Caddas	Wool yarn or tape
Cotton	A woollen cloth
Cruel	Wool yarn or tape
Cut	Slashed fabric in a garment
Edged	Probably a strip along the edges of a garment inside and out. Possibly similar to binding.
Faced	A fur or material lining the cuffs
Flock	Wool refuse from a fleece sometimes used to make cloth
Frieze	Thick winter weight woollen cloth
Fringe	Probably a strip of fringe around the bottom of a garment
Furred	A broad strip of fur up both sides of the front opening of a garment and around the collar.
Galoon	A type of tape
Goad	Usually 4.5 feet. Linear measure of cloth.
Guard	A decorative band or strip on a garment, not along the edge.
Inkle	Linen yarn or tape
Kersey	A woollen cloth probably 2:2 twill.
List	The outside strip of a piece of woollen cloth often with a distinguishing coloured thread. Probably normally cut off before use.
Mortext	The tabulated and analysed body of alpha-numeric data collected from period sources.
Nail	One sixteenth of a yard or 2.25 inches.
Parchment Lace	Passement lace
Pinked	Decoratively cut fabric in a garment
Russet	Undyed, usually grey, summer weight woollen material
Sarsnet	Silk material
Say	A worsted cloth
Selvedge	The long side edges of a piece of woven cloth.
Taffeta	Normally a silk material
Tentors	A machine or frame for stretching cloth by tenterhooks to dry evenly and square.
Thrum	Lose coarse yarn waste [Web] The unwoven ends of the warp [which went through fulling]
Turned	Taking apart and reassembling of garments to put the inside surface, which had been protected from wear and fading, on the outside and hide the worn outside.
Welted	Probably an inserted strip of material along a seam.

---

[87] A more extensive glossary can be found in volume 34.

Appendix 2
The Abbreviated Corpus Key[88]

The Corpus Pictorum or body of illustrations contains those validated period illustrations which show information relating to the common people of England and Wales between 1558 and 1660.

Each illustration is given a Corpus or "CP" reference. The first 4 digits are the Year followed by code letters indicating the reliability of the image, particularly its date. The final numbers and letters in brackets are to distinguish figures in different images in different publications from the same year and with the same level of certainty.

Code Letters:

c: Circa. This applies mostly to undated paintings and sketches of all sorts [oil paintings, wall paintings etc] and plasterwork where other evidence such as the artists dates, history of the building etc provide an estimate of the range of time during which the art work might have been produced. The CP date is the mid point in the range.

d: Derivative. Most derivatives have been discarded as corruptions of the original but very occasionally near contemporary derivatives may show further insight into garments. Derivatives CP numbers relate to the date of the original not the derivative.

ne: No earlier than. Typically this could apply to an undated publication about events on a known date. The illustration could thus have been produced at any time after the event occurred.

nl: No later than. Usually this means that the illustration appears in a publication of that date but could very possibly have been reused from an earlier publication or that there might have been an earlier edition of the work of unknown date or where the presence of the illustration in an earlier lost edition cannot be certain.

nlo: No later than orphan. The picture was published no later than the date given but is not related to the associated text and therefore there is no indication of place of origin or social status of the participants from the text.

r: Reservations. There are reasons to be cautious about the source. Details of the problem with that particular picture will be found by referring to the Corpus Justified entry. This will be found in conjunction with a certainly level letter such as "s" or "nl".

s: Solid evidence that the illustrations come from this date or within a year before.

sr: Solid with reservations. This means that the date is secure but that place or social status may be unsecure. For example prints that may have been produced on the continent from English sketches may contain foreign costume details.

---

[88] The full Corpus and its justification comprises Volumes 27 to 31. The full corpus guide can be found in Volume 1 appendix 2

Series Contents